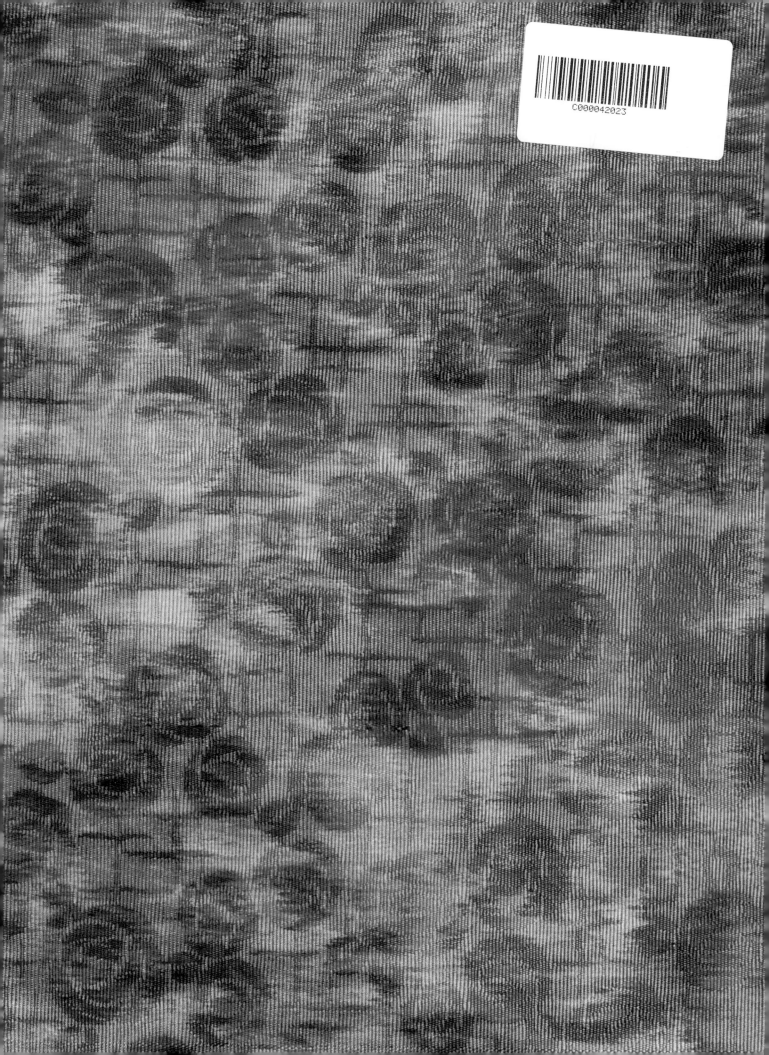

Figural
Japanese Export
Ceramics

Nancy N. Schiffer

Schiffer Publishing Ltd

4880 Lower Valley Road, Atglen, PA 19310 USA

Dedicated to Marvin Baer
with admiration and appreciation

Library of Congress Cataloging-in-Publication Data

Schiffer, Nancy N.
Figural Japanese export ceramics / Nancy N. Schiffer.
p. cm.
ISBN 0-7643-1503-X
1. Pottery, Japanese. 2. Pottery figures--Japan. I. Title.
NK4167 .S35 2002
738.8'2'0952075--dc21
2001005737

Designed by Bonnie M. Hensley
Cover design by Bruce M. Waters
Type set in SloganD/Zurich BT

ISBN: 0-7643-1503-X
Printed in China
1 2 3 4

Published by Schiffer Publishing Ltd.
4880 Lower Valley Road
Atglen, PA 19310
Phone: (610) 593-1777; Fax: (610) 593-2002
E-mail: Schifferbk@aol.com
Please visit our web site catalog at **www.schifferbooks.com**
We are always looking for people to write books on new and related subjects. If you have
an idea for a book, please contact us at the above address.

This book may be purchased from the publisher.
Include $3.95 for shipping. Please try your bookstore first.
You may write for a free catalog.

In Europe, Schiffer books are distributed by
Bushwood Books
6 Marksbury Ave. Kew Gardens
Surrey TW9 4JF England
Phone: 44 (0)20 8392-8585; Fax: 44 (0)20 8392-9876
E-mail: Bushwd@aol.com
Free postage in the UK. Europe: air mail at cost.
Please try your bookstore first.

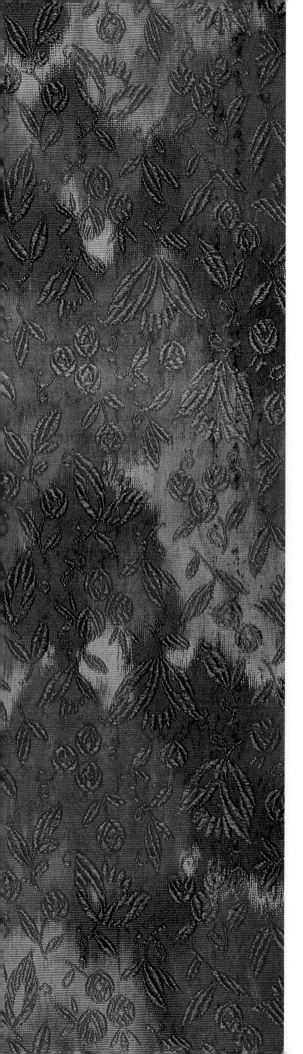

Contents

Acknowledgments _____ 4

Introduction _____ 5

1. Gods of Good Fortune _____ 14

2. Deities and Folk Characters _____ 38

3. Demons _____ 88

4. Children _____ 97

5. Beautiful Women _____ 119

6. Wildlife _____ 160

7. Marks _____ 202

Bibliography _____ 222

Index _____ 223

Acknowledgments

The enthusiam for Japanese arts that Marvin Baer brings to life is infectious. Anyone who meets him is touched by his passion for the objects he studies and loves and is taught something, even some little something, at every conversation. I have been touched by Marvin in numerous ways, as a collector, an admirer, and a writer. The fact that he will part with the items for a price makes them accessible to all. He has enriched me immeasureably and made friends throughout the world. I thank him for inspiring me to carry on my studies with enthusiasm.

Through the network of people who enjoy learning about Japanese ceramics, many collectors have become known to one another and to me. With them I have seen variations of forms I could not have imagined and heard stories about the figures that I could not believe; some I later came to understand, and some I have yet to comprehend. That is the nature of on-going learning and what makes life vigorous, for me. So I must thank each person who has guided me and shared his or her collection with us so that we all may have experiences with these figures and decide what we believe about them. Therefore, I sincerely appreciate the many efforts of the following people for their kindness during the preparation of this work: those who prefer to remain anonymous, Marvin Baer of The Ivory Tower, Inc., Ridgewood, New Jersey; Bonnie Boerer, Hilda and Neal Cohen, Donna Fuller, Shelley Goldberg, Leila Grossinger, Maxine P. Lynn, Aaron and Virginia Messing, Hal Miller, Helen W. Nowell, Lawrence Robbins, Marvin and Nina Vida, and Sandra Wasserman.

Values

The U. S. dollar value ranges provided with the photo captions reflect the market at the time of publication. They have been compiled diligently and conscientiously, taking into consideration variables in the world market and are only intended as a reflection of the current market. No responsibility for their future accuracy is accepted by the author, publisher, or the people credited with the photographs.

Introduction

The study of western trade with Japan is a fascinating field complicated by incomplete primary sources, few eyewitness accounts, and serious language barriers. Archaic terms in each culture must be recognized and attempts to translate them into contemporary vernacular are subjective, at best. Here is a brief summary to acquaint the novice with the field and to invite further study.

Japanese cultural items have been known in select European circles for over four hundred years. Portuguese Jesuit missionaries in the late sixteenth century, Dutch East India Company traders from the first quarter of the seventeenth century, and British East India Company traders from the first quarter of the eighteenth century brought limited knowledge and Japanese goods to Europe. The Dutch company found a market in Europe for the exotic and even crude Japanese ceramics exported by their traders (called "factors") from warehouses (called "factories"), first located on Hirado Island off the northwest coast of Kyushu Island in Japan. In 1641, the Dutch base of operations was moved to Deshima Island near the port of

Figure of a reclining bull and its keeper, 8-1/4" h. *Courtesy of the Drick-Messing Collection.* $1200-1500.

Nagasaki, further south along the western coast of Kyushu. The British East India Company's trade in Japanese ceramics was a significant portion of their activities during the mid-eighteenth century, until English-made ceramics became more widely available at the end of the century.

The Japanese government stifled contact with the outside world throughout the eighteenth and first half of the nineteenth centuries. Diplomatic courtesies were discouraged, and production of goods by Japanese makers was intended for the domestic markets. Only after American Naval Commodore Matthew Perry and his fleet entered Tokyo harbor in 1853 did the Japanese authorities begin to gradually change their views. Over the next fifteen years, events in Japan culminated in domestic reforms and the end of the Edo Period (1600-1868). The Meiji Period in Japan began with a new government in 1868 and extended until 1912.

Japanese business leaders were quick to take advantage of the domestic changes in their country and a few formed private companies to produce hand-made goods for export to the Western markets. A few accepted an invitation to exhibit their goods in Paris in 1862.

The Paris International Exhibition of 1862 brought popular knowledge of Japanese ceramics and other handcrafts to a receptive audience. There, a large and exquisite series of ceramics was shown, where their brilliant red, gold, and soft white ground claimed both attention and admiration. In the wake of the exhibition, a wave of Japonisme invaded Europe, since the main attraction there was the arts and crafts of Japan. Later, exhibitions of Japanese arts in Paris in 1867, 1878, and 1900, Philadelphia in 1876, Chicago in 1893, and Saint Louis in 1904 helped to inform the Western world about Japanese aesthetics, materials, and craftsmanship.

After the new Meiji government was established in Japan in 1868, the leaders made their first priority the establishment of a new society based on capitalistic systems and institutions of the advanced European and American countries. "Growth of productive industry" became a national slogan with which the government led the nation to attain equity with world powers. Western methods of production were introduced, and industries on a modern scale arose quickly. The ceramics industry was no exception. Measures were taken to introduce a new system of production with modern factory equiment, including firing by coal-burning kilns, shaping in plaster molds, and using European glazing methods.

In 1870, the new Meiji government invited a German chemist, Dr. Gottfried Wagener (1831-1892), to teach Arita ceramists in the

European methods. In 1871, he moved on to Tokyo to instruct students at the Kaisai School, the forerunner of Tokyo University. The new generation of ceramics professionals vastly expanded production and the export market to Europe and America. Dr. Wagener became a member of the Imperial Japanese Commission to the 1876 Philadelphia Centennial Exhibition. The Japanese display there included ceramics based in Japanese traditions and made with the modern techniques. The American and European public responded with enthusiasm.

In London by the 1870s, Japanese art in every form was readily available in retail shops, including one run by Arthur Lasenby Liberty. Working with avant-garde painters, including James McNeill Whistler, and writers, including Oscar Wilde, Liberty's shop for Japanese goods of many types became enormously influential to the development of art in England for over fifty years. The Japanese goods there were studied and interpreted by the western art communities that went on to develop new styles of art, including Art Nouveau. Liberty Style is still synonymous with Art Nouveau throughout the world.

In Paris during the 1880s through the 1920s, art dealer Samuel Bing ran an important gallery where he encouraged many artists to appreciate and be inspired by Japanese art works. He is credited with declaring, "Nothing exists in creation, be it only a blade of grass, that is not worthy of a place in the loftiest conceptions of Art... Under such influences the lifeless stiffness to which our technical designers have hitherto so rigidly adhered will be relaxed by degrees, and our productions will become animated by the breath of real life that constitutes the secret charm of every achievement of Japanese art." (Koch, combined edition, p. 59) In the 1880s, Vincent Van Gogh was a frequent visitor to Bing's gallery, where he spent time browsing through Japanese prints. Also, New York artist and businessman Louis Comfort Tiffany entered the gallery in 1889 and struck up a friendship with Bing that lasted many years. Their friendship helped both Tiffany to develop his creativity in the Art Nouveau style and Bing to popularize Tiffany's work in Europe. (*Ibid*) Bing had satellite galleries in New York, London, and Berlin. Tiffany formed a significant collection of Japanese bronze sword guards (*tsuba*), which he displayed proudly over his fireplace in the Tiffany home on Madison Avenue in New York city. The influence of Japanese arts in the West in the late 19th century cannot be overstated.

The most characteristic Japanese export ceramic wares found in American and European markets today are enameled and painted products of the late 18th, 19th, and early 20th centuries.

They include Imari, Hirado, and Kutani porcelain, Satsuma, earthenware, and Banko and Sumida pottery.

Imari Porcelain

Of all the ceramic products of the different provinces of Japan, those made in the Hizen province and known as Imari ware are the most famous. The name is not, however, due to its being made at Imari, but rather because it was shipped from the port of Imari to all parts of the world. In Imari, in fact, there are no potteries. The companies producing the ware, about twenty-five in number, all were situated at Arita, on the sides of Idsumiyama mountain, the "mountain of springs," from which comes the porcelain clay. Decorations on this porcelain are characteristically found in enamel colors and gold. The intense blue color was produced from cobalt.

Imari characters, amusing figure of a woman in a kimono and a man wearing a hat and black boots standing on one foot. 9" h. *Courtesy of MPL and BL collection.* $800-1000.

Hirado two-part helmet incense burner, 5-3/4" h. $2000-2500.

Hirado Porcelain

About six miles to the south of Arita is situated the site of the Mikawachi kiln, which was established from about 1650 by a Prince of Hirado, and the productions of this kiln have commonly been called Hirado ware. This finely made ware originally was produced solely for the use of the Prince and for presentation to his friends. Among the most characteristic of its productions was a porcelain of fine quality decorated in the blue and white fashion, with a number of boys playing under a pine tree; on the choicest pieces are seven boys, but on the less perfect specimens there are only five or three. These, and indeed many examples of Hirado ware, are of small size. Among the few specimens of old Hirado work known are figures of glazed, and partially glazed, porcelain, either white or slightly touched with blue and brown; hanging flower vases, decorated with colored enamels; delicately perforated covers for bowls; and paperweights formed of branches of trees, around which are twined wild flowers. These works afford a marked contrast to later works, which exhibit occasional faults and were made for export.

Three Hirado figures: Hotei with a bag in his head, Daikoku on his bag, and a boy with a lion mask. Each about 4-1/4" h. $800-1200 ea.

Kutani Porcelain

About the year 1650, Godo Saijiro established a kiln at Kutani, in Kaga province, where the clay to make vessels and figures is found. The name Kutani signifies, literally, *the nine valleys*, and it is by this name that the ware generally is known. The ware is often decorated with gold details on a red ground.

Large seated figure of a dignitary, a man with a mustache, Kutani, 1880-1900. *Courtesy of The Marvin Baer - Bonnie Boerer Alliance Collection.* $2500-3000.

Satsuma Earthenware

The province of Satsuma is situated on the south-west end of the island of Kyushu. The manufacture of pottery in this province dates from the latter part of the fifteenth century, but the choicest pieces which reached Europe in the mid-nineteenth century appear to have been produced from early in the eighteenth century to the beginning of the nineteenth by the enlightened Prince of Satsuma. The beautiful, creamy white ware with distinctive crackle glaze for which Satsuma is celebrated is a soft-paste faïence of a firm texture.

In the late eighteenth century, potters in the Kyoto area recreated Satsuma-type ceramics with different clays brought to Kyoto from afar. Fine examples can be found in many forms, including figurines. In the late nineteenth century, Kyoto Satsuma vessels and figurines with thickly applied decorations, primarily for the export market, were made. These are fairly abundant today. The crackle glaze on the Kyoto ware is much smoother than Satsuma province ware, and the decoration is decidedly raised, some being known as *moriage*. Many later Kyoto pieces date from the 1920s and beyond.

Satsuma cottage with removable thatched grass lid, attributed to Jinjukan. 6" h. $2500-3000.

From the left: Old Satsuma earthenware figure of the Chinese warrior Kan Wu, who was distinguished during the restoration of the Chinese Kan dynasty. He usually is identified by the very long beard, which is reputed to have measured four hands. 11" high. Old Satsuma earthenware figure of a goat and tree trunk, probably copied from a European design because the goat is not native to Japan, but the Portuguese and Dutch traders at Hirado Island kept sheep and goats. 10" high. Old Satsuma earthenware figure of a crane and tree trunk. 13" high. Lithograph by Audet for Didot & Cie, Paris, c. 1880. From the James L. Bowes collection, Plate XVIII, Audsley and Bowes, *Keramic Art of Japan*, 1881.

Banko Pottery

The origin of the term Banko for a distinctive earthenware group of the early twentieth century is unclear. The popular term describes a rough, brown or grey clay used primarily for tea implements such as tea pots and vases that are decorated with charming floral and character images.

Sumida Pottery

Kilns were established in Asakusa, near Tokyo, about 1860 on the banks of the river Sumida. Here, vessels and figures with both porcelain and pottery elements were made for export.

Prominent Sumida potters include Ryosai I (born 1828), who came from Seto and worked in Tokyo. He developed the characteristic style in the late 1890s. The pottery clay forms the primary shape, and some elements of decoration are made in porcelain clay. His son succeeded him as Ryosai II (born 1860) and worked at the Tokyo site. The third generation potter, Ryosai III (1888-1971), moved the manufacturing site in 1924 to Yokohama.

The forms are cleverly designed and often humorous, with Japanese-style animals and figures as prominent decorations.

Banko brown pottery figure of seated monkey holding white fruit. 5" h. *Courtesy of MPL and BL collection.*

Square Sumida tea box in the shape of a house with pitched roof and a relief woman figure on the roof. 6" h. *R.B. & G. Collection.* $800-1000.

is believed by the Japanese to have power, by knocking with his hammer, of producing from his treasure bag whatever he requires. The day of the rat is the season at which all classes are most zealous at the shrines of Daikoku.

Satsuma figure of Daikoku with a tied bag and small drum. 4" h. *Courtesy of MPL and BL collection.*

Satsuma box in the shape of a tied bag with lid and five rats on top of Daikoku's bag. 3-1/2" h. *Courtesy of MPL and BL collection.* $1000-1200.

Daily Food * Yebis

Yebis (Ebisu), is of Japanese origin and is shown, with large ear lobes, as a fisherman. The vocation of fisherman was much respected among the old Japanese; fish and rice were to them what meat and bread have been to Western nations. Yebis was the sun god Tensio Daisin's brother, but by him disgraced and banished into an uninhabited island. He could live two or three days under water. Therefore, he is the Neptune of the country and the protector of fishermen and sea-faring people. Often Yebis is shown sitting on a rock with an angling-rod in one hand or the celebrated dorado fish in the other. He is usually represented as a short, stout figure, with a happy and humorous expression, dressed in loose garments, wearing on his head the black cap. Sometimes he slips along on the back of a fiend-like dolphin. A figure of Yebis is to be found in almost every house.

At Nishinomiya, between Osaka and Kobe, is the chief temple to Yebis's honor in Japan. The temple is frequented by merchants and artisans who have need to pray for daily food and goods the gods can give. The twentieth day of the tenth month is the great annual festival of Yebis.

Opposite page: Kutani figure of Daikoku and Yebis two men dancers, one with drum and black boots and one with fan and bare feet. 9-1/4" h. *Courtesy of MPL and BL collection.*

Satsuma seated man with fan, marked Yebis. 3-1/4" h. *Courtesy of MPL and BL collection.*

Two Imari figures of standing gods Yebis, in white cloak and holding large orange fish and bag, and Daikoku in dark cloak cleaning his ear. 10-1/2" h. *Courtesy of MPL and BL collection.* $800-1200.

Kutani figure of a standing fisherman god Yebis, with red fish. White raised scroll decoration on his clothing. Rocky brown base. 11-1/4" h. *Courtesy of MPL and BL collection.*

Contentment * Hoteï

Hoteï, the god of contentment, of Chinese Buddhist origin, is a contented spirit in the midst of poverty. Without home, fire, or other domestic comforts, he leads a roaming Bohemian life, wandering about with a wallet or sack, sometimes full, but more often empty. He sits down among his special friends, little children, telling them amusing stories. Hoteï is usually represented as a squat, stout figure, with a large belly, which is generally freely exposed by the scantiness of his attire; his head is uncovered, and he generally carries a sack, fan, and lamp. Sometimes he is depicted seated on a buffalo, and at others on a sack of hemp. Hoteï is a dreamy, yawning, obese vagabond and a prodigious favorite with country folk.

Large Imari Hotei figure with sack, fan, and detailed face. 14-1/2" h. *Courtesy of the Drick-Messing Collection.* $1200-1500.

Satsuma and Imari style Hotei figures, for comparison. 13-1/4" h. *Courtesy of the Drick-Messing Collection.*

Satsuma Hotei figure seated with tied bag and fan. 2-3/4" h. *Courtesy of MPL and BL collection.*

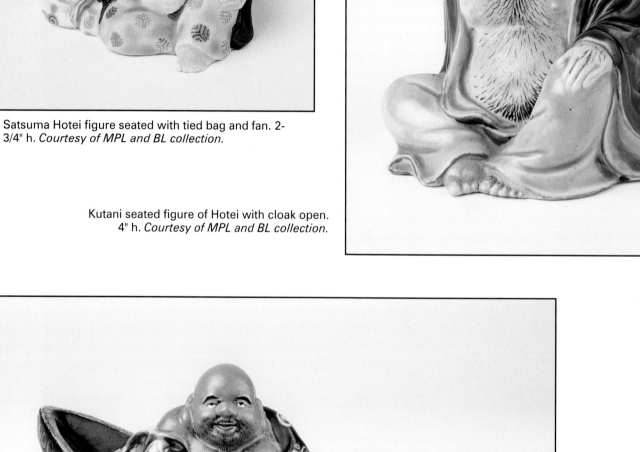

Kutani seated figure of Hotei with cloak open. 4" h. *Courtesy of MPL and BL collection.*

Kutani boat with removable Hotei lid. 8-1/4" l. *Courtesy of MPL and BL collection.*

Kutani figure of Hotei with robe open, holding bag. 9-1/2" h. *Courtesy of MPL and BL collection.* $700-900.

Kutani figure of Hotei with tied bag and fan, gourd and walking stick. 5-1/4" h. *Courtesy of MPL and BL collection.* $500-600.

Imari figure of Hotei as a Kabuki actor, man wrapped up in his sack and holding a fan. 4-3/4" h. *Courtesy of Marvin and Nina Vida.* $300-500.

Small Hotei figure with moriage raised decorated kimono, child figure, and fan at his head. *Courtesy of the Drick-Messing Collection.*

Scholar * Fukurokuju

Fukurokuju (Toshi-Tokû) is of Chinese origin and the scholar, doctor, god of wisdom, genius, and talents. He is accessible to little children to inspire them in all sensible amusements that require both thinking heads and skillful fingers. He is represented as a grave and amiable old man, clad in an ample gown with long sleeves and stole, attended by a stork or a fawn, carrying a fan and a long staff on which are suspended his manuscripts. The developed upper portion of his head is accompanied by large ears and sharp eyes. He is a perpetual wanderer, distributing as he goes his precious gift of knowledge. He is specially worshipped at the New Year.

Satsuma figure of Fukurokuju, the god of wisdom, standing with shepherd's crook and hat. All-over raised moriage scroll decoration, c. 1930s. 12-1/4" h. *Courtesy of MPL and BL collection.* $500-600.

Satsuma figure of Fukurokuju, the philosopher diety, with white beard holding left arm over his head. 5-1/4" h. *Courtesy of MPL and BL collection.*

From the left: Bizen stoneware figure of Fukurokuju (Toshi-Toku), 9.5" high; Kyoto stoneware figure of Girogin attributed to Takahashi Dohachi, 10" high. From the James L. Bowes collection, Plate XXXII, Audsley and Bowes, *Keramic Art of Japan*, 1881.

Womanhood * Benten

Benten (or Benzaiten) is of Hindu origin as the godess of love, beauty and wealth. She is not the goddess of mere physical beauty and sensual love, but rather perfect womanhood. She is generally represented seated, in a contemplative mood, sometimes on a dragon, running her fingers over a biwa, a kind of stringed instrument. As the personification of the sea, she is frequently represented standing or sitting on the seashore. When she is depicted without the instrument, she carries in one hand a key, and in the other the priceless pearl, and is richly attired in a blue mantle, with the sacred stole, and wears a royal headband. She is worshipped on a far higher plane as the principle of virtue personifying the nourishing ocean that provides, feeds, and enriches. "The Japanese encircle her beautiful brow with a divine aureola, crown her head with an imperial diadem, and clothe her in magnificent robes...Benten is always the mother,...generator, provider, educator;...and completest embodiment of the virtues and deeds most useful and pleasurable to man." (Jarves, as quoted in Audsley and Bowes, p. 100)

In certain representations of the goddess at Buddist temples, Benten displays eight arms, with hands bearing emblems of her many good offices. Her head is adorned with three celestial flames. In this form she is the protecting genius of mother earth, the dispenser of all those gifts which promote its fertility. She is the giver of all the comforts and blessings which make life charming. Women of all creeds pray to Benten for attractiveness, ability and riches; and men seek her aid to enable them to become wealthy by the exercise of their genius. The snake is her messinger and held sacred to Benten, and the day of the snake is her special time. Worshippers are careful not to injure reptiles, for fear of experiencing the anger of Benten and the consequent refusal to their petitions.

Glory * Bishamon

Bishamon (or Bishamonten), the god of war and glory, the king of men, the personification of all knightly virtues, is of Hindu origin and patron of princes and warriors. He is not a popular deity, for war seldom brings blessings to the tradesman or laboring man. Bishamon frequently empties their purses, destroys the fruit of their toil, and burns down their houses. Bishamon is also the heavenly protector of the priestly class. He is represented as a warrior fully clad in rich armor, often with a pagoda in his right hand and a lance adorned with streamers in his left hand .

Opposite page: Satsuma figure of Benten standing with right arm held across her body. 5-1/4" h. *Courtesy of MPL and BL collection.*

Satsuma 3-part tea caddy with Bishamon seated on lid. 12-3/4" h. *Courtesy of The Marvin Baer - Bonnie Boerer Alliance Collection.* $2500-3000.

Satsuma seated figure of Bishamon holding a pagoda lantern. 3-3/4" h. *Courtesy of MPL and BL collection.* $1800-2000.

Kagoshima province Satsuma figure of Bishamon, god of wealth and power, in Gosu blue colors, seated warrior holding a pagoda. 3-5/8" h. *Courtesy of MPL and BL collection.* $1500-1800.

Sumida figure of Bishamon standing in dark cloak holding a stick, monkey with a pagoda at his feet. 9" h. *Courtesy of MPL and BL collection.* $1200-1500.

Chapter 2
Deities and Folk Characters

Deities

Buddhist drawings of deities are frequently found on vases, bowls, hanging pictures, in books and scrolls, and as ceramic figures. The god of the wind is represented as a grotesque monster. The god of thunder is another grotesque creature, half-man, half-beast, depicted leaping about amidst dark clouds and striking, with the sticks he carries in his hands, a ring of drums that encircles his head. The god of war is a figure with three heads and many arms, which wield different weapons, such as the bow, sword, and spear. He is depicted rushing through the air or standing on the back of a wild boar or a wild horse.

Gama-Sennen, or the frog saint, has a Chinese origin, and is an emblem of long life.

Kannon (Kwan-on) is of Chinese Buddhist origin and the compassionate deity of mercy. Sometimes Kannon is shown wearing a crown or tiara and riding an elephant or lion. Some representations show Kannon with many arms.

Okami is the goddess of theater, usually shown as a stout figure.

Daruma is a bulging-eyed character wrapped in a red robe holding a Buddhist fly whisk. He was a priest and teacher of Zen Buddhism who went to China and sat in meditation so long that he lost the use of his legs. One day he fell asleep, which upset him so much that he cut off his eyelids so they would never close again. From his discarded eyelashes sprang up tea plants.

From the left: Kyoto stoneware figure of a Buddhist Sennen, man of wisdom, riding a fish and holding a book, 12.5" high. From the James L. Bowes collection, Plate XXXII, Audsley and Bowes, *Keramic Art of Japan*, 1881.

Therefore, he is associated with serving tea, especially to scholars and literary men.

Rakan (or Arhats) are the eighteen followers of Buddha, usually represented as skinny old men. They have individual identities, but are generally grouped and known for their wisdom.

From the left: Bizen stoneware figure of a Buddhist Sennen (man of wisdom), 9-1/4" high; Bizen stoneware figure of a dragon coiled around bamboo, 19" high; Bizen stoneware figure of Fukurokuju, 9-1/2" high. From the James L. Bowes collection, Plate XXXI, Audsley and Bowes, *Keramic Art of Japan*, 1881.

Hirado figure of a warrior riding a boar, and perhaps representing the god of war. 3-3/4" high. $1000-1200.

40

Kutani figure of Gama-Sennen seated with a frog on his shoulder. 10" h. *Courtesy of MPL and BL collection.* $800-1000.

Opposite page: Very heavy solid cast Kutani figure of the Japanese god of thunder and lightning, kneeling devil man in red skin with hair standing up and fangs, holding a pipe and a string of five drums with beaters on the second cloud base. Long fingernails and toenails. 11" h. *Courtesy of MPL and BL collection.* $1800-2000.

Very heavy Satsuma figure of Gama-Sennen as an old man with grey beard and walking stick, seated on a huge frog with rough brown skin. 11" h. *Courtesy of MPL and BL collection.* $3500-4000.

Opposite page;
Top: From the left: Kyoto stoneware figure of Gama-Sennen, 8.5" high; Kyoto stoneware figure of a shishi (lion), 9.5" high. From the James L. Bowes collection, Plate XXXII, Audsley and Bowes, *Keramic Art of Japan*, 1881.

Bottom: From the left: Bizen stoneware figure of a crane, 9-1/4" high; Bizen stoneware figure of Daikoku seated with two rice bags. 13-1/4" high; mid-17th century Ohokawachi earthenware figure of the mythical Chinese frog saint, Gama-Sennen, who is known in Japan as a symbol of long life, 8-5/8" high. From the James L. Bowes collection, Plate XXXI, Audsley and Bowes, *Keramic Art of Japan*, 1881.

Satsuma figure of seated deity Kannon, c. 1875-1880. 11" h. *Courtesy of The Marvin Baer - Bonnie Boerer Alliance Collection.* $2500-3000.

Imari figure of the Buddhist deity of mercy, Kannon, standing with a layered kimono, crossed hands, and necklace, c. 1790-1820. 22" h. *Courtesy of The Marvin Baer - Bonnie Boerer Alliance Collection.* $6000-7000.

Satsuma figure of Kannon seated on an
elephant, gilded surface. 8" h. *Courtesy
of MPL and BL collection.* $2500-3000.

Kutani figure of Kannon holding a stick and sitting on a shishi's back, dark mane and tail, green fur. 7-1/2" l. *Courtesy of MPL and BL collection.* $900-1000.

Imari figure of Okami, goddess of the theater, with a drum. 8-1/4" h. *Courtesy of The Wasserman Collection.* $1000-1200.

Opposite page: Imari figure of the goddess of the theater, Okami, crouching with a bundle on her back, c. 1870. 6" h. *Courtesy of MPL and BL collection.* $600-700.

Imari figure of Okami seated in white floral kimono holding a fan. 6-1/4" h. *Courtesy of MPL and BL collection.* $400-600.

Satsuma figure of Daruma sleeping on a curled tiger, glazed bottom open. 2-1/2" h. *Courtesy of MPL and BL collection.* $1000-1200.

Kutani figure of Daruma with white flowing staff, red cloth, and fly whisk. 7" h. *Courtesy of MPL and BL collection.* $275-375.

Kutani figure of Daruma reclining in a red cloth cloak with his fly whisk. 3-3/4" h. *Courtesy of MPL and BL collection.* $300-500.

Large Kutani figure of seated Daruma holding a fly whisk with white wool over his shoulder and gilded figure in his palm. 13" h. on gold lacquered base, 3-1/4" h. *Courtesy of MPL and BL collection.* $2200-2500.

Fine figure of a seated Buddhist sage. 7-3/4" h.
Courtesy of The Wasserman Collection. $800-1000.

Sumida Buddha being painted by two artists. 9-1/4" h. $2500-3000.

Imari standing figure of the Japanese Buddhist rendition of Christ, man with facial hair, robe open, tightly curled hair. 16-1/2" h. *Courtesy of MPL and BL collection.* $1500-1800.

Folk Characters

In the ceramic wares made in Japan, figures of noted warriors and heroes, clad in their armor of steel and silk, are gorgeous in appearance, but usually stiff and angular.

Theatrical figures are clad in fantastic garments, sometimes imitating butterflies or birds. Figures of people from court life often show nobles or ladies clothed in the stiff and many-folded brocade costumes of ceremony.

In figures of wrestling athletes, muscles are invariably represented unnaturally developed. Men wrestling, playing practical jokes upon one another, or engaged in games of amusement or skill, are frequently depicted naked, or almost so, not for the love of the nude, but simply because the artist saw naked men engaged in such occupations before his eyes every day.

Kutani figure of seated man with helmet and quiver. 8" h. *Courtesy of MPL and BL collection.*

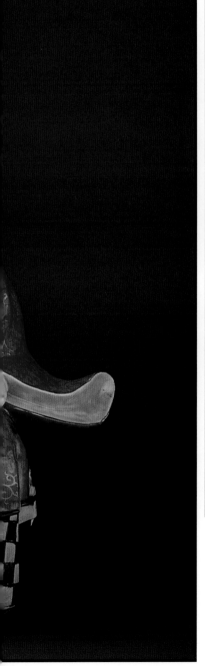

Pair of Kutani figures of seated professor and student, late 19th century, c. 1890-1900. 13-1/2" h. *Courtesy of The Marvin Baer - Bonnie Boerer Alliance Collection.* $6000-7500.

Satsuma figure of seated man with Samurai armor and fan on scrolled base, open at bottom.
8-1/2" h. *Courtesy of MPL and BL collection.* $2000-2400.

Figure of a theater dancer with celadon robes, red wig, gold mask, made by Fukagawa with paper label on base. 9" h. $1000-1200.

Kutani standing Kabuki theater figure with bowl and ladle, long red hair. 12-3/4" h. *Courtesy of MPL and BL collection.* $1100-1400.

Imari figure of two Kabuki dancing boys with drum and fan.
6-1/2" h. *Courtesy of MPL and BL collection. $800-1000.*

Imari figure of a standing Kabuki actor with fan and hand over head, red kimono. 8-1/2" h. *Courtesy of Marvin and Nina Vida.* $500-700.

Imari figure of a Kabuki actor as a seated boy in red robe, c.
1930s. 7-1/2" h. *Courtesy of Marvin and Nina Vida.* $400-500.

Imari figure of a Mikado dancer with
fan and gold head ornament. 11" h.
Courtesy of MPL and BL collection.
$800-1000.

Opposite page: Kutani figure of
kneeling Mikado actor man with fan
raised to his head, dark blue robe, 8-
1/4" h. *Courtesy of MPL and BL
collection.* $600-800.

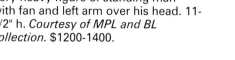

Very heavy figure of standing man with fan and left arm over his head. 11-1/2" h. *Courtesy of MPL and BL collection.* $1200-1400.

Pair of small figures of seated theater characters dressed as a Samurai and courtesan. Man with sword and woman with elaborate gilded headdress. 2-1/4" h. *Courtesy of MPL and BL collection.* $1000-1200 the pair.

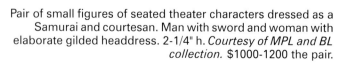

From the left: Hirado porcelain figure of a member of the Mikado's court seated with a fan in his hand; Hirado porcelain figure of a Buddhist sage lost in contemplation and blind to the things of the world. Plate X, Mew, *Japanese Porcelain*, no date (about 1915).

Kutani figure of a standing man blindfolded, with hands raised in front of him. 9" h. *Courtesy of MPL and BL collection.* $600-800.

Kutani figure of standing man with white hair, from the streetsweepers couple, holding a wooden rake. 8-1/4" h. *Courtesy of MPL and BL collection.* $400-500.

Imari figure of an old woman from the streetsweepers couple, holding a broom. 7-1/2" h. *Courtesy of MPL and BL collection.* $400-500.

Kutani figure of standing old woman with long grey hair, from the streetsweepers couple, holding a broom. 9" h. *Courtesy of MPL and BL collection.* $500-600.

Kutani double vase with the legendary characters Ashenaga and Tenaga. 12-1/2" h. *Courtesy of The Marvin Baer - Bonnie Boerer Alliance Collection.* $3000-3500.

19th century Hongo pottery (Iwashiro province) figure of a squatting man on a raised stool, and with removable basketry hat and bowl. Plate XIV, Mew, *Japanese Porcelain*, no date (about 1915).

Satsuma figure of a standing man in white robe with fan and left hand held over his head. 14" h. *Courtesy of MPL and BL collection.* $3500-4000.

Ceramic standing figure of a man in white robes holding fruit. 8-1/4" h. *Courtesy of MPL and BL collection.* $2500-3000.

Kutani figure of seated man holding a pipe and case. Green kimono, resting on a bundle of twigs. 9-1/4" h. *Courtesy of MPL and BL collection.* $700-900.

Figure of a man with a bale and a cat at his feet, hollow cast. 9" h. *Courtesy of the Drick-Messing Collection.* $1000-1200.

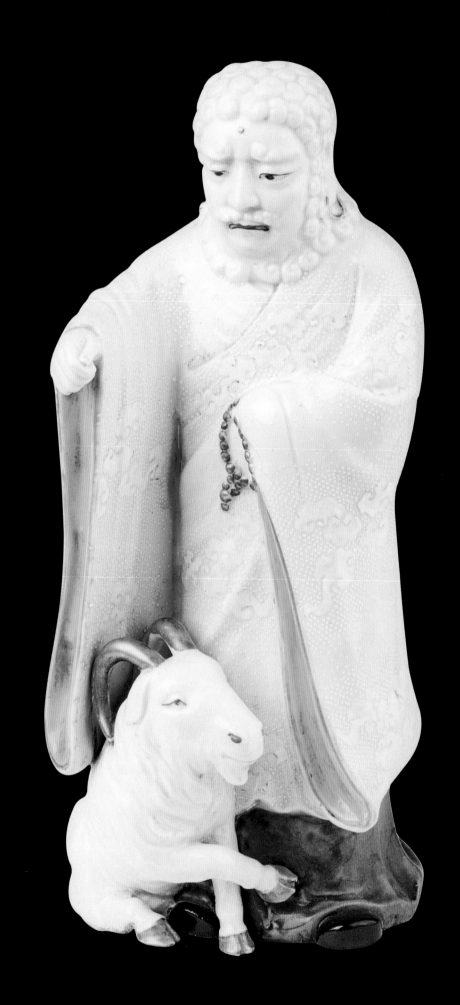

Opposite page: Satsuma figure of a standing man in white kimono holding a gourd, green leaf on head, c. 1930. 11-1/2" h. *Courtesy of MPL and BL collection.* $1200-1500.

Imari porcelain standing figure of a man, green cap and floral robes. 10-1/2" h. *Courtesy of MPL and BL collection.* $800-1000.

Imari figure of standing man with layered kimono tied with a belt. 9" h. *Courtesy of MPL and BL collection.* $800-1000.

Exquisite Satsuma seated figure of woman
seated on a bundle of sticks by Jinjukan. 8-1/2"
h. $4500-5000.

Satsuma seated figure of woman seated on a bundle of sticks by
Jinjukan. 8-1/2" h. *Courtesy of The Marvin Baer - Bonnie Boerer
Alliance Collection.* $4500-5000.

Satsuma figure of woman sitting on a bundle of sticks with scarf on her head, dark cloak, holding writing sticks, by Jinjukan. 8-3/4" h. *Courtesy of MPL and BL collection*. $4500-5000.

Sumida wrestling men, labeled Taimano Keimaya with mark.
6-3/4" h. *Courtesy of the Hilco Collection.* $1500-2000.

Sumida wrestling men with impressed mark of Ishigaro Koko, 6-1/2" h. and mark. $1500-2000.

Sumida Suma wrestling men, 6-1/4" h. $2000-2500.

Satsuma figure of an acrobat tumbling on a drum, dragon face in his head ornament. 7" h. *Courtesy of MPL and BL collection.* $1800-2000.

Chapter 3
Demons

Demons (Oni) of the nether world are portrayed in Buddhist works of art as being painted red, blue, green, or some other rich color, which very materially adds to their infernal aspect. They often have the head of an ox or a horse and are sometimes tusked and horned.

The demons of the earthly world, by contrast, can take on animal forms and sometimes appear as inanimate objects. Therefore, a demon could turn himself into a vessel of oil, and thereby manage to enter a home where he might make trouble.

Shoki is the demon killer.

Early 19th century Seto porcelain figure of Shoki with a demon under his foot, back inscribed under the glaze "Made by Shin-bei, at the age of 65. Seto. Plate II, Mew, *Japanese Porcelain*, no date (about 1915).

Large pottery figure of a demon (Oni) with dark skin straddled over the god Shoki, shown crawling. Cast open at the base, 1865-75. 16-1/2" h. *Courtesy of MPL and BL collection.* $4000-4500.

On the subject of demons, the Buddhist Inferno can be divided into four sections. The first section has three human figures, dressed in grave clothes, finding their way from a dark valley towards a direction-post which marks the ford of a mighty rushing river. The valley and the river are emblems of death and the grave, the cold passage towards the world beyond. Far on the bank is seated a terrible gray-headed giantess resting against the trunk of a dead tree, grinning in a fearful manner at a group of four miserable beings kneeling at her feet. From them she is removing the grave clothes before she allows them to proceed on their journey. Almost naked they have now to appear before the dread judge who is to pronounce their awful punishment.

In the second section, the judge, a huge red giant, is seated behind a table, upon which is spread a page of the book of records. He holds in his right hand a sort of club or bat, a blow from which frightens his culprits or emphasizes his remarks. To his left, are two assistants and a blue demon, horned, tusked, and holding a ponderous mace; on the right of the judge is a recording scribe, with a brush and a tablet covered with writing.

Hirado figure of Shoki fighting a dragon. 5-1/2" h. $2000-2500.

The third section presents an awful phase of punishment; this is the section of blood. In it is found the numerous wretched sinners beaten to pieces with a club, torn by carrion birds, cut and tortured with stake and knife, crushed between huge rocks, and pounded in a mortar with an immense spiked pestle. The horror of these punishments is increased tenfold to the Buddhist by the belief that at every infliction the body is restored, to experience fully the recurring torture.

The last division is the section of flame, the most fearful and imaginative of the series in which whirlwind, lightning and fire struggle for the mastery, and combine to torture the lost in their dreadful agony. It represents the final pit called "Eight times deep"—a vast whirlpool of lurid storm, broken by awful streams of blood-red lightning—the whole scene viewed through raging flames. On the outer edge writhe serpents, ever watchful to prevent escape.

Kutani figure of a demon with horns and cloth bag and Okami in
blue kimono with rectangular box. 10-1/4" h. *Courtesy of MPL
and BL collection.* $1200-1400.

Kutani figure of Shoki, the Oni (devil) killer, standing in white robe with black beard and sword. 11-1/4" h. *Courtesy of MPL and BL collection.* $1200-1500.

Kutani figure of Shoki standing with
a sword and long black hair. 13" h.
Courtesy of MPL and BL collection.
$1000-1200.

Kutani figure of Shoki with a young woman cleaning his ear.
9-1/2" h. *Courtesy of MPL and BL collection.* $1000-1200.

"Japanese devils do not seem to be the enemies of men like the orthodox Christian demon. They have a marked preference for playing tricks with their bodies, and getting out of them while in the flesh all sorts of impish entertainment. The aboriginal devils roast their victims by coarse jokes and pointed jeers. Sometimes the living men, by the aid of superior spirits, get the better of these devils, and turn the laugh on their teasers and frighteners." (Jarves as quoted in Audsley and Bowes, page 105)

A Kutani figure of a girl cleaning the ear of Shoki. Fine quality decoration. 9-3/4" h. *Courtesy of Marvin and Nina Vida.* $800-1000.

From the left: Takatori stoneware figure of Daikoku, 7.25" high; mid-17th century Ohokowachi stoneware figure of Tetsksai, an imaginary character, 12" high; 17th century Ohokowachi stoneware figure of Shoki slaying the demon, 6" high. From the James L. Bowes collection, Plate XXXII, Audsley and Bowes, *Keramic Art of Japan*, 1881.

Chapter 4
Children

Children are shown in Japanese figures engaged in a variety of activities, including playing games such as shuttlecock, making snowballs, writing calligraphy, spinning tops, and blowing soap bubbles. They are seen in figures with their pets: cats frequently, and with dogs, monkeys and frogs less often. Young mothers or servants appear with small children.

Hirado figure of Kishimojin, a female deity from China, who protects children and women in childbirth. She is usually shown standing, holding a baby toher bosom, and with the Flower of Happiness in her right hand, or sitting surrounded by children. 6-3/4" h. $3500-4000.

Imari figure of a man and two boys, 10" h. *Courtesy of The Marvin Baer - Bonnie Boerer Alliance Collection.* $1200-1500.

Opposite page: Kutani figure of a small boy with a drum and Hotei as a lion dancer, 9-1/2" h. *Courtesy of MPL and BL collection.* $600-800.

Figures of young boys usually are depicted with heads almost entirely shaved, except for tufts of hair here and there. Armor expresses a boy's ambitions to become a great and renowned warrior. The Feast of Boys, held in May, inspires images of paper carp attached to poles outside a house and flying free in the air. Iris leaves and a small wooden sword are used as emblems of this feast.

Kimono with very long sleeves were worn only by young girls, and this is an indication of the age of the person represented. It also shows she is not married. When a young man and woman are shown in art works sharing an umbrella, this suggests they have been living together without telling their parents. When green plums are shown in a design, it is an indication that a young lady is pregnant. The subtleties of Japanese art are endlessly fascinating.

Hirado porcelain group of five children playing blind man's bluff. Frontispiece, Mew, *Japanese Porcelain*, no date (about 1915).

Hirado barrel vase with three boys in the foreground. 8-1/2" h. $3500-4000.

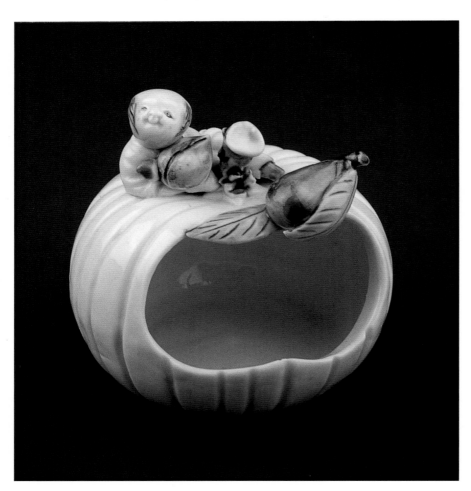

Hirado melon-shaped bowl decorated with eggplant and seated boy on top. 3" h. $1500-2500.

Three Hirado figures of seated children: a pair flanking a globe, a boy with a fan, a boy with a lion's mask. each about 2" h. $800-1200 ea

Sumida figure of two boys on a red wagon, by Ryosai. 7-1/4" h. *Courtesy of The Marvin Baer - Bonnie Boerer Alliance Collection.* $1200-1500.

Large Imari figure of a boy holding a ball and seated on a board for the game of Go. Plate VII, Mew, *Japanese Porcelain*, no date (about 1915).

Imari figure of a boy with a drum. 9" h. *Courtesy of MPL and BL collection.* $800-1000.

Figure of a young boy with black drum and metal head piece, Imari, c. 1880-1890. 9-3/4" h.
Courtesy of The Marvin Baer - Bonnie Boerer Alliance Collection. $1250-1800.

Imari seated boy with drum and painted kimono, front and back. 9-1/2" h. *Courtesy of Marvin and Nina Vida.* $600-800.

Imari boy with red drum, , c. 1880-1890, 7-1/2" h $500-800; and seated Imari
boy with green bird, c. 1880-1890. 8-1/4" h. *Courtesy of The Marvin Baer -
Bonnie Boerer Alliance Collection.* $1500-1800.

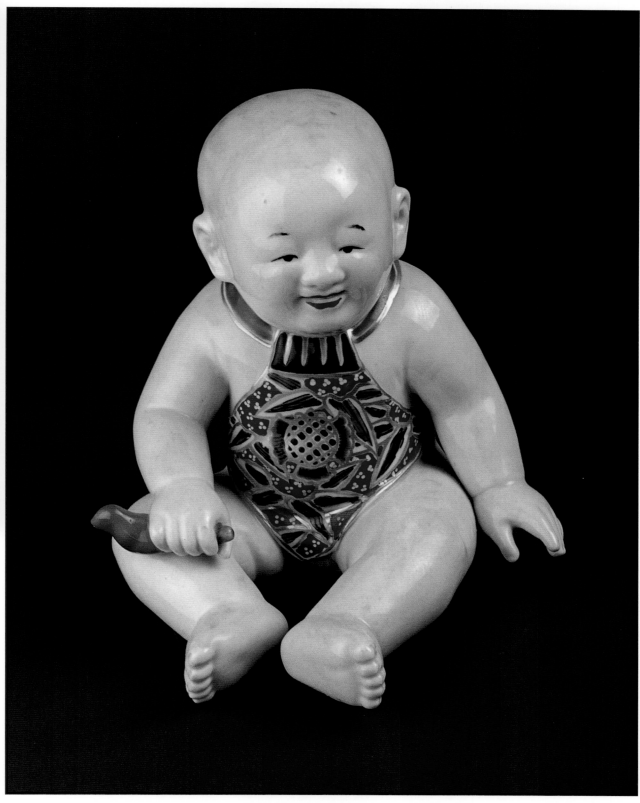

Two similar Satsuma standing boy figures, one holding a dog and the other holding a shell or rock, elaborately decorated floral and gilded robes. 6-3/4" h. *Courtesy of MPL and BL collection.* $1200-1500 the pair.

Miniature Satsuma boy figure by Jinjukan. 3-3/4" h. *Courtesy of Marvin Baer, The Ivory Tower, Inc.* $1000-1500.

Satsuma figure of standing boy with lion head mask. 11-1/2" h. *Courtesy of The Marvin Baer - Bonnie Boerer Alliance Collection.* $3500-4000.

Satsuma covered rectangular casket with pierced lid and peacock orb finial, two standing boys at sides. Front of casket with painted scene of a dragon and two figures in a raging sea, back painted with landscape including a horse and people, unsigned, c. 1870-1880. 14-1/2" h. *Courtesy of The Marvin Baer - Bonnie Boerer Alliance Collection.* $10,000-12,500.

Hirado seated boy with melon. 5-1/2" h. $2000-2500.

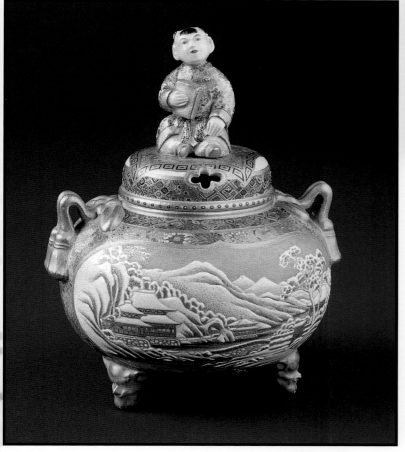

Large Satsuma covered bowl with boy on lid and a footed base, winter landscape on one side and a parade of people on the other, by Taizan, c. 1880. 6" d. $4500-5000.

Girls and young women are traditionally shown by Japanese artists to be reading and representing the Six Accomplishments, which were considered important in their development toward womanhood: etiquette, music, archery, horsemanship, calligraphy, and arithmetic. Girls also may be represented depicting the Five Virtues: charity, dutifulness, courtesy, judgment, and fidelity; and sometimes depict the Four Classes: samurai, farmer, artist, and merchant. For example, girls can be shown as lady samurai, rice planters (farmer), print makers (artist), and fan sellers or print sellers (merchant). The Feast of Girls is in March, and the special flower connected with it is the cherry blossom. Dolls often ornament the houses during these festivities. Girls might be seen arranging fifteen special dolls on a stand of five or six tiers.

Kneeling girl in floral kimono. *Courtesy of MPL and BL collection.* $600-800.

Imari incense burner in the shape of a girl, perhaps young Okami, holding a bowl. 3-1/2" h. *Courtesy of Marvin and Nina Vida.* $300-400.

Heavy Satsuma figure of a standing girl with large, closed fan showing a man in relief on the end, in cobalt blue kimono with gold floral decoration. 12-1/4" h. *Courtesy of MPL and BL collection.* $4000-4500.

Kutani standing woman with rectangular screen and seated girl holding a scroll. 10-1/2" h. *Courtesy of MPL and BL collection.* $600-900.

Imari figure of seated girl holding a scroll of writing, green-draped stool. 8-1/2" h. *Courtesy of MPL and BL collection.* $600-800.

Chapter 5
Beautiful Women

Figures of women in Japanese ceramics are nameless lovely women used to create a lovely mood. Women are frequently shown with, and are artistically compared to flowers, to express the many aspects of feminine beauty.

Kutani figure of kneeling woman with orange kimono and two brown drums. 8" h. *Courtesy of MPL and BL collection.* $600-800.

Late Kutani, c. 1930s, fine quality figure of a standing woman. 13-3/4" h. *Courtesy of Marvin and Nina Vida.* $700-900.

Kimono were often long in front so that a woman moving about held up the front part. The kimono sash, the obi, and intricate and variously shaped bow, the obijime, are important parts of an artistic design. All obi were originally tied in front, but changes in fashion in the mid-eighteenth century changed that. The width of the obi is important. In the early eighteenth century, the obi was only about three or four inches wide. Then it became fashionable to wear an obi two feet wide folded over double. Later, a more informal obi about ten inches wide or a little less, was introduced.

A long underdress frequently had a differently colored lining which showed brightly when the hem was turned back. Styles of the kimono collar and cuffs also changed through time and are variously reflected by the taste of the artists depicting them.

Women of different sizes and shapes are represented in the figures. Some are shown with tiny hands, but one cannot be certain that was the artist's intention. Some have beautiful arms with stubby fingers and badly formed wrists. No generalities can be made. Variations can be noted in facial features and cultural types.

Peasant women are usually shown wearing woven sandals made of bamboo sheaths on a straw sole.

It is not usually possible to determine the age of a woman depicted in a figure. Sometimes older women are represented without eyebrows and with two v-shaped marks over the nose to denote wrinkles.

Imari figure of a small standing woman with arm up, good modeling and painted. 7-1/2" h. *Courtesy of Marvin and Nina Vida.* $500-700.

Imari figure of woman with fan and left hand raised. 8" h. *Courtesy of MPL and BL collection.* $600-800.

Imari standing figure in a dark blue kimono, holding fan, base broken out. 14" h. *Courtesy of MPL and BL collection.* $1200-1400.

Large figurine of woman with green kimono. 26" h. *Courtesy of Marvin Baer, The Ivory Tower, Inc.* $2400-3000.

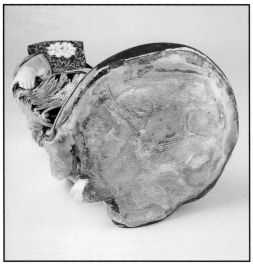

Imari standing woman with fan raised, fine detail on back. 17-3/4" h. *Courtesy of MPL and BL collection.* $2000-2400.

Imari figure of woman in blue kimono with fan. 13". *Courtesy of Marvin and Nina Vida.* $800-1000.

Imari dancing woman in green flowered kimono, 10-1/2" h. *Courtesy of Marvin and Nina Vida.* $800-1000.

Women are shown in figures in their roles as mothers, teachers, farmers, waitresses at a tea house, and geisha. The tea house had a powerful influence on the community. In the early days, a man could not have access to his chosen courtesan without recourse to the services of the tea house. In time, it became customary for a visitor to be entertained while awaiting the courtesan, and the type of entertainment was an indication of the status of the visitor. Eventually, the tea house became the site of freelance entertainers and dancers who were called *geisha* in Tokyo and Osaka and *geiko* in Kyoto (*ko* was a diminutive ending of female names).

To become a geisha, a young Japanese girl was trained to provide entertainment and lighthearted company, especially for a man or group of men. Some were singers, dancers, and other pleasant entertainers. In 1799, all geisha were required to obtain a license from the local government, and this gave them a professional status they have never lost.

Geisha are shown in ceramic figures not to represent an individual entertainer, but rather the role of the job. They are known by their dress and its accessories, their behavior, the way the clothes are worn, and their gestures and stance. They show the theatrical nuances between joy and sorrow, moving seamlessly back and forth in a characteristic stylishness. That is geisha; a mood of gaiety and amiability are typical.

Geisha were attended by a manservant who carried a box and sometimes a lantern. Occasionally a maidservant carried the lamp, and then both servants would appear.

Geisha rarely wear their family crest (*mon*) on their kimono, except at New Year festivities. They generally tie the obi behind, and have less elaborate hair ornaments than the courtesan. Out of doors in summer, geisha wore a single thronged sandal and in the winter, high clogs (*geta*). Apprentice geisha of Kyoto traditionally wore the high, lacquered, black clogs.

Imari figure of a lady holding a bowl. Plate XII, Mew, *Japanese Porcelain*, no date (about 1915).

Two Imari women gazing up, one in black robe and one in blue robe. 10" h. *Courtesy of Marvin and Nina Vida.* $1200-1500 the pair.

Kutani figure of woman standing holding a dog. Purple kimono. 10-1/2" h. *Courtesy of MPL and BL collection.* $600-800.

Kutani figure of kneeling woman in purple kimono, playing with a cat. 8" h. *Courtesy of MPL and BL collection.* $500-600.

Kutani figure of crouching girl and cat with cloth ball, c. 1890. 5-1/4" h x 7-1/2" l. C*ourtesy of the L. Robbins Collection.* $1400-1600.

Kutani figure of woman holding a dog with string obi tied at the back, 11" h., and tiny Kutani cat, c. 1860, 2-1/2" l. *Courtesy of MPL and BL collection.* $600-800.

Imari figure of woman holding a cat, 19-1/2" h., and tiny figure of a dog. $3000-3500.

Imari figure of lady with dog, string obi tied in back. 11-1/4" h. *Courtesy of MPL and BL collection.* $800-1200.

Imari figure of seated lady
holding a dog, blue kimono.
8-7/8" h. *Courtesy of MPL
and BL collection.* $600-800.

Kutani figure of standing woman in orange kimono, repaired, holding a cat. 14-1/4" h. *Courtesy of Marvin and Nina Vida.* $1200-1400.

Fancy standing woman with long kimono with gold fan, two gold combs in long hair. 12-1/2" h. *Courtesy of MPL and BL collection.* $1000-1200.

Courtesans (Bijin) were companions to courtly, wealthy, and upper-class men in the early times. Later, they were connected with the idle samurai, rich merchants, actors, and artists at teahouses. In the ceramic figures of courtesans, the interest of the design centers on the hair, face, and kimono. Many of the gestures have vaguely alluring suggestions, such as the withdrawal of arms inside the kimono, frequently heightened by stray, disordered strands of hair at the sides on their temples. Courtesans wear heavy, white-lead, theatrical face make-up, generally giving them a flat look when depicted.

The ever-changing patterns and colors of the fabrics of their kimono provide endless interest to their images. Only courtesans regularly wore the obi bow in the front; all other women usually tied it in the back. This detail can distinguish the courtesan. They are seldom shown with footwear, since they traditionally had bare feet. In winter, though, they usually wore the high clogs (*geta*), and are so depicted.

Over the years, certain dances and songs have beacome associated with courtesans. The "Daikoku-mai" song is one, derived from one of the dancers who wore the mask of the god of riches, Daikoku. Dances, such as the Niwaka dance, also are associated with courtesans.

Standing woman with hands clasped and held up. 11-1/4" h. *Courtesy of MPL and BL collection.* $800-1000.

Tall standing woman with left arm propped
on her hip and right arm holding up her skirt,
in dark blue kimono with floral decoration.
17" h. *Courtesy of MPL and BL collection.*
$1800-2000.

Tall standing woman with left arm propped on her hip, and right arm holding up her skirt, kimono with bird decoration. 16-1/2" h. *Courtesy of MPL and BL collection.* $1400-1600.

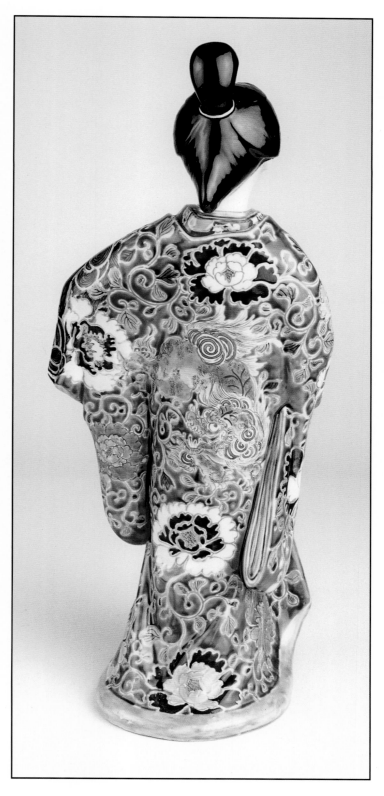

Similar Imari woman with green kimono, floral decoration. Inside obi and red neck band. 16-3/4" h. *Courtesy of Marvin and Nina Vida.* $1200-1500.

Similar Imari standing woman in white kimono. 17" h. *Courtesy of MPL and BL collection.* $1800-2000.

Imari standing figure of courtesan
in blue floral kimono and obi with
gold phoenix. 15-1/2" h. *Courtesy
of the L. Robbins Collection.*
$2000-2500.

Imari figure of a standing courtesan with winter kimono raised to show five overlapping kimono. Well painted. Obi tied in front, 15" h. *Courtesy of the Drick-Messing Collection.* $3000-3500.

Imari figure of woman holding round bowl with red and gold petal exterior. Chrysanthemums on kimono. 9-1/2" h.. *Courtesy of MPL and BL collection.* $800-1000.

Heavy Imari figure of standing woman holding a bowl, hair with four pins. 13-1/4" h. *Courtesy of MPL and BL collection.* $1200-1400.

Satsuma woman in white kimono holding a vase. Elaborate hair decoration. 23-1/2" h. *Courtesy of MPL and BL collection.* $3500-4000.

Imari woman holding a yellow vase
with green dripped glaze. 15" h.
Courtesy of MPL and BL collection.
$1500-1800.

Imari woman with red box, 20th c. Taisho period. 9-1/2" h. *Courtesy of MPL and BL collection.* $500-600.

Imari standing figure of a woman with gourd hanging over her shoulder, white hat. 14-1/4" h. *Courtesy of MPL and BL collection.* $700-900.

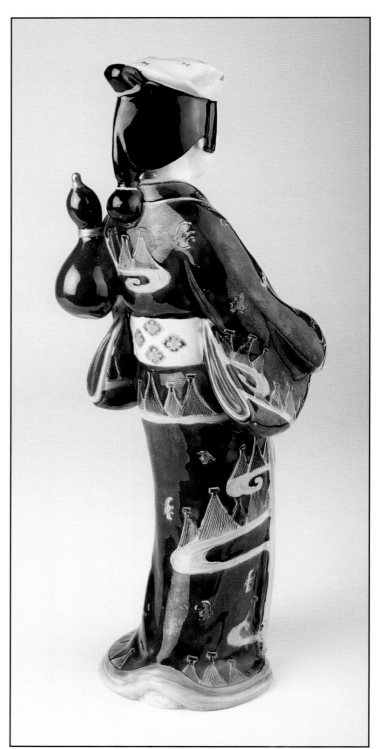

Imari standing woman holding a doll, gold dots in kimono with all-over floral decoration. 11-1/2" h. *Courtesy of MPL and BL collection.* $1000-1200.

Kutani 20th c. figure of kneeling woman in dark kimono with white dog. 7-1/4" h. *Courtesy of MPL and BL collection.* $600-700.

Kutani kneeling woman with dog. 7" h. *Courtesy of Marvin and Nina Vida.* $600-700.

Late Kutani, fine quality, standing female dancing figure with gold detail and fan. Floral relief decoration, c. 1930s. 17-3/4" h. *Courtesy of Marvin and Nina Vida.* $1800-2200.

Late Kutani dancing figure with gold detail, different decoration and hair, c. 1930s. 17-3/4" h. *Courtesy of Marvin and Nina Vida.* $1800-2200.

153

Imari figure of a standing woman with blue kimono and fan next to her head. 11-3/4" h. Mounted as a table lamp. *Courtesy of Marvin and Nina Vida.* $600-800.

Seated woman on silk pillow and bench. 11-1/2" h. *Courtesy of Marvin and Nina Vida.* $800-1000.

Imari figure of Okami as an older
woman holding a red facial mask.
11-1/2" h. *Courtesy of Marvin and
Nina Vida.* $800-1000.

Kutani figure of two standing women
with dark skin, one holding a yellow
vessel. 10-1/4" h. *Courtesy of The Ivory
Tower Inc., Ridgewood, New Jersey.*
$900-1200.

Kutani mother and daughter or teacher and student reading a book. 7-1/4" h. *Courtesy of Marvin and Nina Vida.* $600-800.

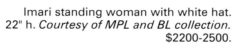

Imari standing woman with white hat. 22" h. *Courtesy of MPL and BL collection.* $2200-2500.

Kutani figure of kneeling woman in pink kimono. She is holding flowers. 6-1/4" h. *Courtesy of MPL and BL collection.* $300-500.

Imari standing figure in blue kimono. 11-1/2" h. *Courtesy of Marvin and Nina Vida.* $800-1000.

Kutani standing woman with fan and right hand held to her ear, elaborately decorated robes. 11" h. *Courtesy of MPL and BL collection.* $800-1200.

Kutani figure of woman holding green straw hat and scarf on her head. 10-1/4" h.. *Courtesy of MPL and BL collection.* $600-800.

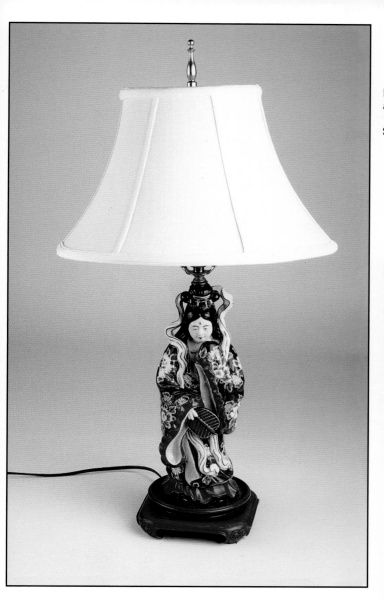

Kutani figure of a standing girl, mounted as a lamp with the fixture rising from her hair. 12-1/4" h. *Courtesy of Marvin and Nina Vida.* $600-800.

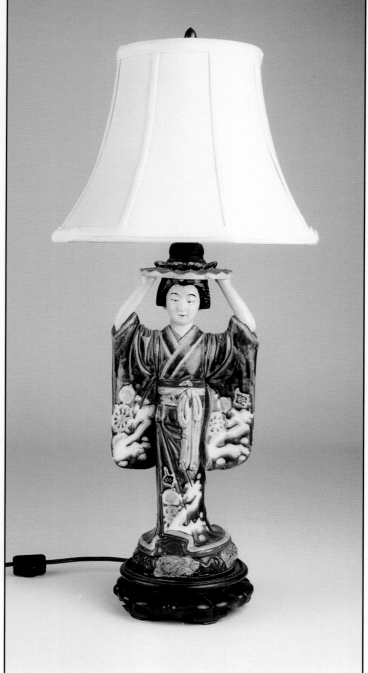

Imari figure of a girl in a green kimono holding a round tray over her head, red obi. 13-1/2" h. Mounted as a table lamp. *Courtesy of Marvin and Nina Vida.* $500-700.

Chapter 6
Wildlife

Animals

Four-footed beasts, either wild or tame, are scarce in Japan. A survey of Japanese art shows that of all natural objects, quadrupeds are the least frequently depicted. Of all the larger quadrupeds, the horse is the greatest favorite and the animal most frequently drawn by Japanese artists. Other animals found in figures of Japanese ceramic art include the oxen, deer, bears, dogs, cats, rabbits, rats, and frogs. Cranes, tortoises, fir trees, and bamboos are accepted emblems of longevity.

Cats are numerous in Japanese ceramic figures, especially Kutani sleeping cats. They have been associated with geisha and courtesans, perhaps because they, too, prowl at night. They are said to have been used outside a door to indicate that a room was occupied.

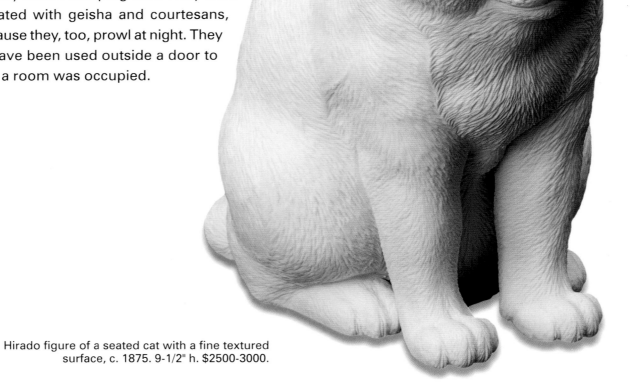

Hirado figure of a seated cat with a fine textured surface, c. 1875. 9-1/2" h. $2500-3000.

Hirado figure of a standing cat with arched back. 3-1/4" h. $600-800.

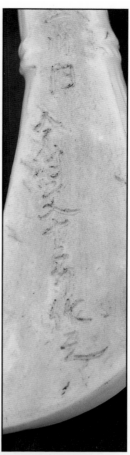

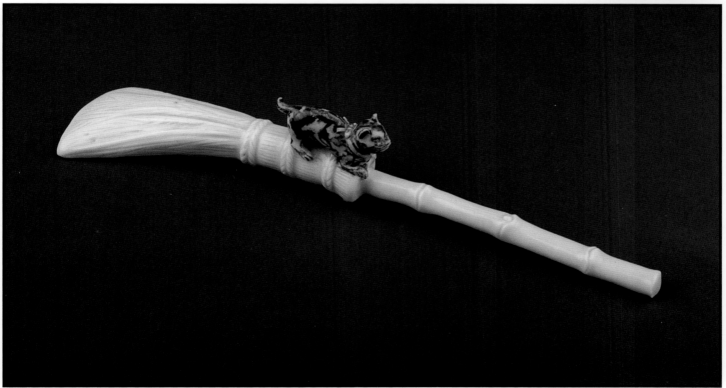

Hirado brush rest, figure of a broom and kitten, back inscribed (above). 6-1/2" l. $2000-3000.

Satsuma covered box by Yabu Meizan on four mice with cat finial on lid. 5" h. $15,000-20,000.

Tiny Kutani cat. 2-1/2" l.. *Courtesy of MPL and BL collection.* $150-200.

Two Kutani cats. 6-3/4" and 3-3/4" l.. *Courtesy of MPL and BL collection.* $500-700 and $300-500.

Large Kutani cat. 12-1/2" l.. *Courtesy of MPL and BL collection.* $1200-1400.

Black Kutani cat, 6" l., and tiny white Kutani cat. *Courtesy of MPL and BL collection.* $300-500 and $150-200.

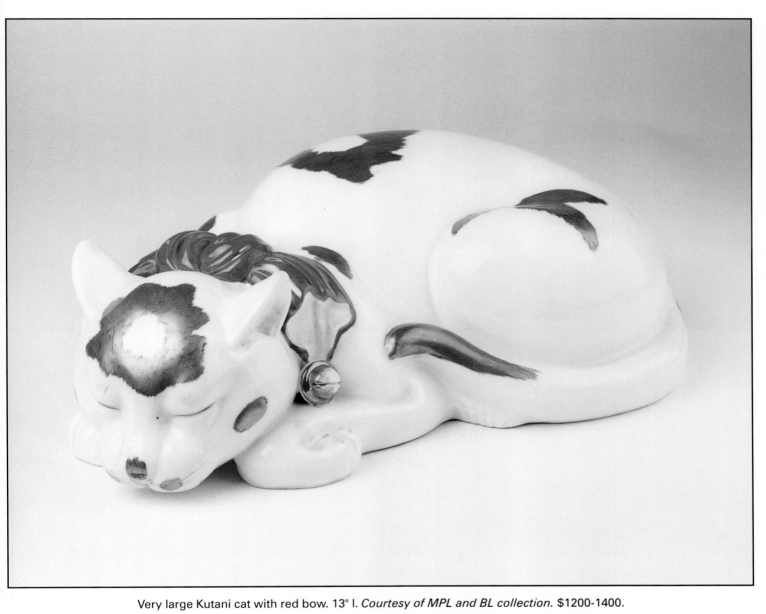

Very large Kutani cat with red bow. 13" l. *Courtesy of MPL and BL collection.* $1200-1400.

Kutani cat. 9-1/4" l. *Courtesy of MPL and BL collection.* $600-900.

Two Kutani cats. 7-1/2" l., with red tie and two bells. $500-700. 5" long, with red tie and two bells. $500-600

Kutani cat, with gold and brown fur. 5-1/2" h. *Courtesy of the Hilco Collection.* $1000-1200.

Kutani cat with red bow and two gold bells. 9-1/2" l. *Courtesy of MPL and BL collection.* $700-900.

Seated Kutani beckoning cat with painted brown fur, raising his left arm. Red ruff around neck. 5-3/4" h. *Courtesy of MPL and BL collection.* $600-800.

Later seated Kutani beckoning cat, c. 1930s, with raised left paw, raised decoration on red ruff, and green bow. 12" h. *Courtesy of MPL and BL collection.* $300-500.

Brown seated cat with turquoise enameled eyes, bristle whiskers, and white claws. Incised hair. 5-3/4" h. *Courtesy of MPL and BL collection.* $800-1000.

Deer are an emblem of long life in Japan, and a favorite decorative motif representing swiftness and grace.

Dogs are symbolic of domesticated animals and are representative of fidelity and future prosperity.

Hirado figure of reclining deer with relief flower, scroll and leaf ornamentation. 3-1/2" h. $400-600.

Kutani figure of a dog with red neck ruff. 3-3/4" h. *Courtesy of MPL and BL collection.* $400-600.

Hirado white dog standing on four legs, with black eyes. 5" h. *Courtesy of MPL and BL collection.* $1000-1200.

Hirado dog figure seated and scratching with his back foot. 5" h. $1000-1200.

Satsuma pair playful dogs painted brown and black. 4-1/2" h. *Courtesy of MPL and BL collection.* $2500-3000.

The elephant is a Buddhist emblem for strength, and is copied from Indian art. Elephants are not naturally found in Japan.

Elephant figure with blue decoration. 7" h. *Courtesy of The Wasserman Collection.* $800-1000.

Sumida candlestick in the shape of an elephant,
glazed green with a child reading a book on its
back. 6.85" h. *R.B. & G. Collection.* $1500-1800.

Hirado horse. 12" h. $4000-5000.

A horse is a Buddhist emblem of speed, and has been often depicted in Japanese art.

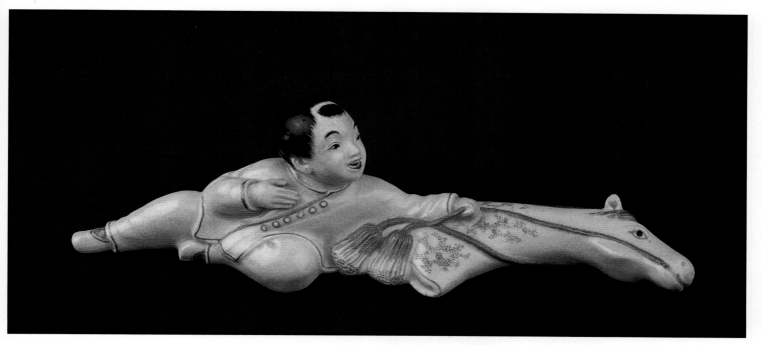

Satsuma brush rest figure of reclining child and horse head. 6-1/4" l. $1000-1200.

From the left: Bizen stoneware figure of a horse jumping over a gourd, probably made to burn perfumed oil, 10.5" high; Tamba stoneware figure of a lion, 14" h.; Bizen stoneware figure of two shishi fighting, 7.75" h. From the James L. Bowes collection, Plate XXXI, Audsley and Bowes, *Keramic Art of Japan*, 1881.

The Japanese *kirin* (or Chinese *kylin*) is a mythical animal no doubt derived from the lion, since the proportions point to the lion as the original source. According to the mythical tradition, only one *kirin* existed at any set time. There are no lions in the Japanese islands.

Imaginary animals of Japanese legends: 1. Dragon with clouds. 2. The *kirin* depicted on earth with a rock and tree and below its stellar constellation which is above the cloud. 3. The *kylin* represented as a lion or *shishi*. 4. The *kait su*, an imaginary animal. 5. The *ho-ho* bird. Lithograph from J. Akerman, London, c. 1880. From the James L. Bowes collection, Plate VIII, Audsley and Bowes, *Keramic Art of Japan*, 1881.

The word *shishi* signifies a lion and represents the natural lion, not a fabulous beast, which is the *kirin*. The *shishi* is frequently introduced in Buddhist subjects, sometimes along with the elephant.

Hirado crouching lion with blue fur details, very early. 3" h. $2000-2500.

Satsuma Koro with large shishi finial, two scenes: men jousting and man
standing. 15-3/4" h. *Courtesy of Marvin Baer, The Ivory Tower, Inc.* $2000-2500.

Early Satsuma incense burner with shishi finial on pierced lid. Cylinder body on three legs. 7-1/2" h. *Courtesy of MPL and BL collection.* $4500-5000.

Large Kutani figure of a shishi and ball with elaborate incised
design . 12-1/4" h. *Courtesy of Marvin and Nina Vida.* $800-1000.

Satsuma figure of a spotted shishi with drum and pierced lid with finial of a boy with a drum and two drumsticks. 4-1/2" h. *Courtesy of MPL and BL collection.* $1500-1800.

Pair of Satsuma shishi incense burners with drum and boys. 6" h. *Courtesy of The Marvin Baer - Bonnie Boerer Alliance Collection.* $2500-3000.

Imari shishi with orange and blue floral decoration, 3-3/4" h. *Courtesy of The Wasserman Collection.* $500-600.

Studio porcelain figure of two wrestling shishi with light green celaden glaze, c. 1900. 6-1/2" h. $1000-1200.

Kutani figure of two fighting shishi, c. 1920s. 4" h. $300-500.

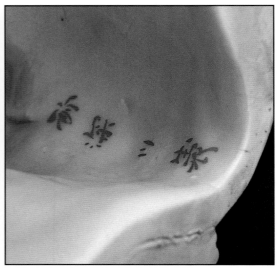

Imari blue shishi with gold details and rare gold Koransha mark. 7-1/4" h. $1500-2000.

Satsuma figure of three shishi at play, c. 1865-75. 5-1/2" h. *Courtesy of the L. Robbins Collection.* $3500-4200.

The monkey, being practically a biped, is generally depicted in that capacity in Japanese art works. The monkey's power and impulse to mimic man make him a favorite artistic subject. Monkeys or apes show the greatest skill displayed in their representation. On works of porcelain and pottery, the monkey is sometimes introduced in the form of a grotesque, such as with unnaturally long arms.

Kutani porcelain figure of seated monkey in blue floral vest, holding fruit above its head. 9-3/4" h. *Courtesy of MPL and BL collection.* $600-800.

Deep Sumida bowl of green glaze with relief monkeys and a plum branch on the rim. 9.25" d. x 5" h. $1000-1200.

Sumida inkwell in the shape of a seated monkey, head is the lid. 3-1/4" h. $500-800.

Hirado monkey and hawk. 7" h. $2500-3000.

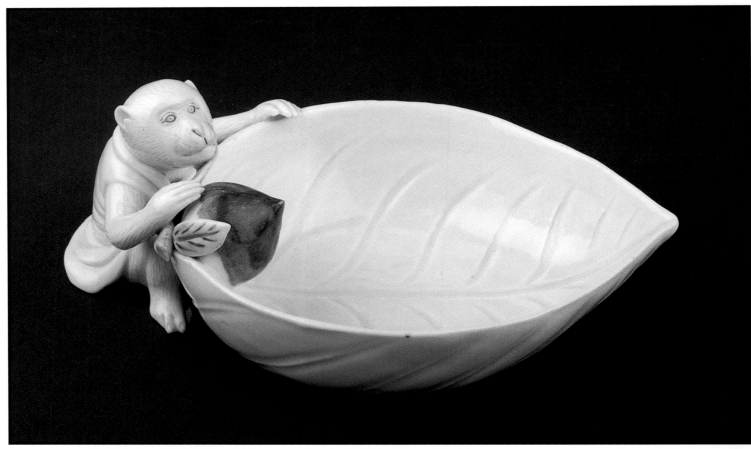

Hirado leaf-shaped dish with monkey and blossom figure. 6-1/4" l. $2000-2200.

Hirado figure of an otter on a leaf. 4" h. $800-1200.

Imari pig incense burner. 8" l. *Courtesy of The Wasserman Collection.* $800-1000.

Kutani rabbit figure with gold and raised hair. 5-1/2" h. *Courtesy of MPL and BL collection.* $500-700.

Birds

Birds usually appear in Japanese art alone or in conjunction with vegetation. The birds most frequently represented are the crane, tame and wild ducks, wild goose, peacock, pheasant, raven, hawk, falcon, and ordinary domestic fowls.

Japanese peacocks, taken from a woodcut. Lithograph from J. Ackerman, London, c. 1880. From the James L. Bowes collection, Plate X, Audlsey and Bowes, *Keramic Art of Japan*, 1881.

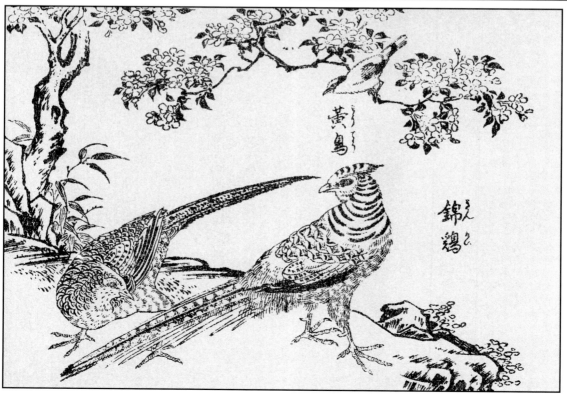

Japanese pheasants, taken from a woodcut. Lithograph from J. Ackerman, London, c. 1880. From the James L. Bowes collection, Plate X, Audsley and Bowes, *Keramic Art of Japan*, 1881.

190

Domestic fowls are often depicted by the Japanese artist, the cocks (roosters) being the greatest favorites. Cocks are commonly kept in temple grounds because they foretell changes of the weather. By the regularity of their crowing, they mark the passage of time.

Satsuma cock (rooster) sitting on a covered drum with a four-leg ged stand. 10-1/2" h. *Courtesy of MPL and BL collection.* $3500-4000.

Japanese cranes, taken from a woodcut. Lithograph from J. Ackerman, London, c. 1880. From the James L. Bowes collection, Plate X, Audsley and Bowes, *Keramic Art of Japan*, 1881.

The crane is held in veneration and is, on account of its supposed long life, very generally accepted as an emblem of longevity. The Japanese avoid representing it as dead; a dead crane would hardly be expressive of longevity.

Sumida figure of white crane, attributed to Koji. 7" h. $800-1200.

Sumida vase as a
bamboo stem with a
standing white crane,
impressed Hara mark.
7.5" h. *R.B. & G. Collection.* $1800-2000.

Ducks of several varieties are portrayed. The beautiful drake and duck, when represented together, are accepted by the Japanese as the emblems of conjugal felicity.

Eagles and falcons do not appear on works of ceramic art nearly as frequently as cranes and other birds, but pheasants, because of their multi-colored plumage, are great favorites of the painters.

The mythical bird *ho-ho* is the most refined and beautiful of all the artist's creations. It is a bird of rich plumage, furnished with a superb tail of long waving feathers. This is a great favorite with Japanese artists, who depict it with elegance and gracefulness. The belief is that the *ho-ho* dwells in the higher regions of the air, out of the sight or knowledge of man, and descends to earth only at the birth of a great warrior, philosopher, or lawmaker who is to exercise an important and beneficial influence upon the country. Its head, body, and wings do not differ in most of its representations, but its tail is seldom found alike. Sometimes the tail closely resembles natural feathers, at others it appears as an elegant flowing mass of conventional scrollwork. When two birds are represented together, it usually happens that their tails are differently designed.

Japanese ducks, taken from a woodcut. Lithograph from J. Ackerman, London, c. 1880. From the James L. Bowes collection, Plate X, Audsley and Bowes, *Keramic Art of Japan*, 1881.

Imari porcelain figure of an eagle. Plate XI, Mew, *Japanese Porcelain*, no date (about 1915).

194

Sea Life

In Japanese artwork, fish are often depicted. A carp ascending a waterfall is a subject frequently met with in Japanese ceramics. It is more commonly represented than any other fish, being a particular favorite of the native artists.

The octopus, or devil-fish, is also depicted on vessels and figures.

Small Sumida vase with octopus at rim. 3" h. $400-600.

Hirado brush rest figure of a merman with green tail, 5-1/2" l., and a Hirado clam shell with crab, 2" l. $1500-2000.

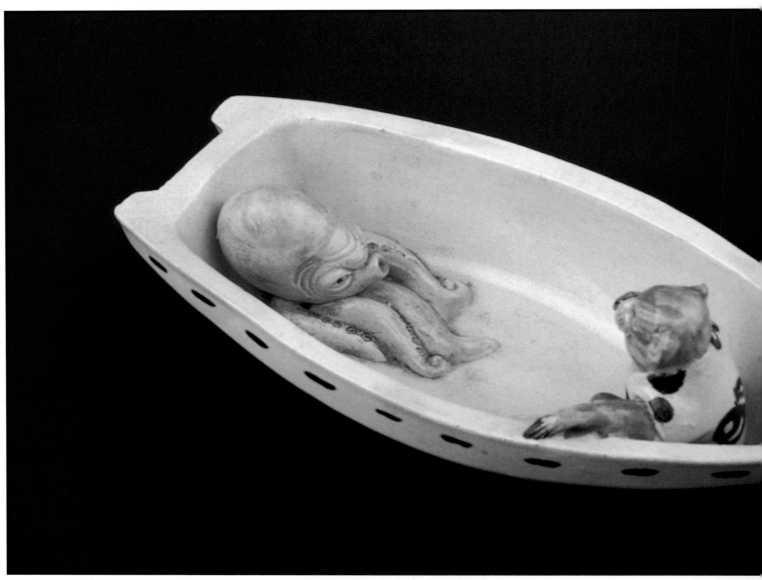

Satsuma boat form enclosing a
monkey and a squid. 5" l. $600-800.

Fukagawa shell-shaped dish with crab.
7-1/4" l. $1500-2000.

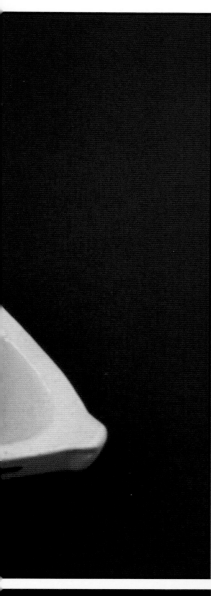

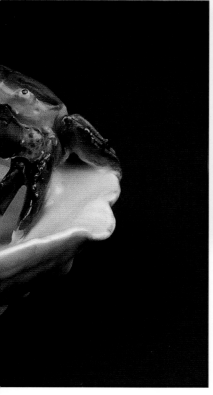

Hirado triple vase of tree trunks and fish by blue sea. 4-1/2" h. $3500-4000.

Reptiles and Insects

Reptiles and insects are truthfully represented whenever they appear in Japanese art. They are unusual in ceramic figures.

The most famous mythical reptile is the dragon, whose's body is long and snake-like in its proportions, covered with scales, and furnished with rows of prominent pointed spikes along its back. The four legs are likewise scaled, and armed with spikes on the outside of the joints. The feet, divided into three members, terminating in curved claws, are represented as very muscular and supple. Its head, derived from a serpent head, has been elaborated to look fearful. The eyebrows are formidable and long flexible horns grow from the sides of the nose. The mouth is open with pointed teeth. The dragon is believed to exert a potent influence over important and national events connected with emperors and heroes. Histories of Japanese gods and heroes are full of fabulous stories of this animal. Flame-like appendages of the dragon are also given to this creature. It is believed to be an animal of good omen, and of such extreme gentleness, that, although gifted with great swiftness of foot, it will swerve from its direct path to avoid injuring an insect or crushing a leaf.

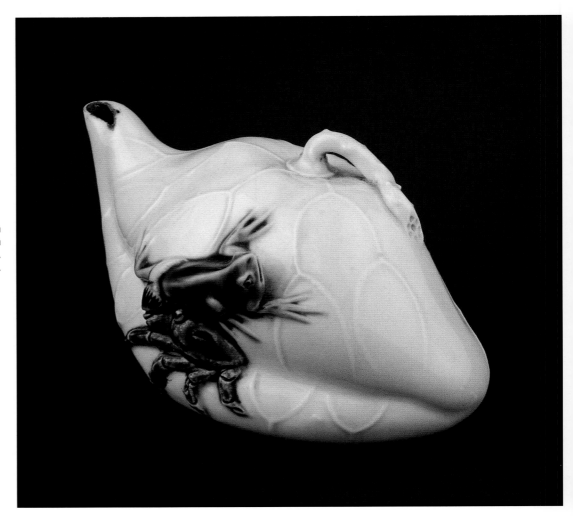

Hirado white water dropper in the form of a collapsed melon with frog and crab at the side. 2" h. $800-1000.

Satsuma figure of a red dragon and Kannon standing on a rocky base with swirling seawater. 9-1/4" h. *Courtesy of MPL and BL collection.* $3000-3500.

The tailed tortoise differs only from the ordinary tortoise by the addition of a long hairy appendage or tail. This creature is not believed to be endowed with any supernatural gifts. The Japanese believe that the tortoise lives for several hundreds of years. They have accordingly accepted it as an emblem of longevity. The tail indicates great age, and is supposed to grow only after the lapse of centuries. The emblematic tortoise appears in Japanese ceramics on dishes, teapots, bottles, and tasteful ornaments, such as figurines.

Hirado Netsuke with a brown and a white spider in relief. 1-5/8" l. $800-1200.

Hirado bisque turtle with crouching man with box. 7-1-4" h. $3000-3500.

Twelve symbols have evolved in Eastern cultures to represent chronological sequences. In popular jargon, the symbols are the signs of the zodiac and their animal representatives denote the years. "Every Chinese knows well under which animal he was born. It is essential that he should do so, for no important step throughout life is taken unless under the auspices of his particular animal. " (Yetts: *Symbolism in Chinese Art*, p. 21 as sited in Williams, p. 412)

The Japanese people have adopted this system of denoting years by the names of animals as follows:

Symbolic Animals	Zodiacal Signs
Rat	Aries
Ox	Taurus
Tiger	Gemini
Hare	Cancer
Dragon	Leo
Serpent	Virgo
Horse	Libra
Goat	Scorpio
Monkey	Sagitiarius
Cock	Capricorn
Dog	Aquarius
Boar	Pisces

Top: Five Hirado bisque figures: a cow and the zodiac emblems dragon, boar, horse, and goat, each about 1-1/2" h. $200-300 each.

Bottom: Four Hirado glazed figures: a lion and the zodiac emblems snake (serpent), dog, and goat, each about 1-1/4" h. $200-300 each.

DAI NIPPON—GREAT JAPAN.

The following three words: *Fuku, Roku* and *Fiu,* together signify Good Fortune.

Fuku, meaning prosperity, luck, and so forth.

Another form of *Fuku.*

Roku, meaning happiness.

Fiu, meaning, longevity.

Another form of *Fiu.*

Banko Pottery

Impressed on Banko ware. *Banko*, the name of the ware.

Impressed. Another form of the word *Banko.*

Painted on the ware, but this method is seldom used. *Ban-ko.*

Impressed *Gan-do Gin Zo*, meaning, made by Gando Gin. The small square marks signify *Banko*, and the larger one is the monogram of the maker.

Impressed *Ban-ko Senshu Yo-fu ken*, meaning, Banko made at the Yofu factory; the word Senshu signifies permanency

Impressed *Yo-fu ken Shu-zin*, meaning, that the article was made by the Master of the Yofu factory. The character at the foot of the stamp is the monogram of the maker

Impressed. The upper mark is *Ban-ko,* and the lower one, *Nippon, Yu-han;* the whole meaning that the article is Banko ware, made by Yuhan, in Japan

Impressed. *Mori uji*, meaning, the Mori family, by whom the article was made.

Hizen Province and Imari Porcelain

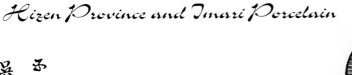

Made by Gorodayu Shonzui 1510-1550.

Used on old specimens of Sakaida Kakiemon 1540-1660.

Zoshuntet Sampo sei about 1825

Mark of the Koransha Company

Orchid mark

Mark of the Kameyama Kiln, near Nagasaki 1803

Yo = porcelain. An old Nabeshima mark

KOSAN-JIN. A Nabeshima mark found on old specimens.

K.A. Found on old Nabeshima porcelain

The sparrow-chain mark on fine Nabeshima porcelain

The comb-chain mark on bases of Nabeshima porcelain used early eighteenth century

Used at Arita about 1800

203

Made in Arita. Floral design in red indicates overglaze (red) painters in Edo Era, 1615-1868. The paper label reads: "Geo. Neighbour & Sons. London." - presumably a retail business.

Fukagawa Porcelain Manufacturing Co, Ltd., late Meiji and Taisho, c. 1895-1925, blue.

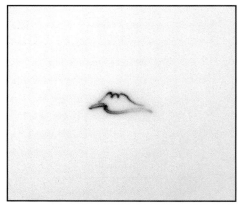

E Gami Sei Toh Sho (the company name) in Arita, Izumiyama area, after middle Meiji Era.

Dai Ming Manreki Nen Sei (the company name), Arita, judging from the writing style the logo is the work of an artisan.

Fukagawa trademark, Fuka (mountain) Gawa (river), blue

Koran Sha Fukagawa, orchid mark of the Company of the Scented Orchid, founded in 1875, red.

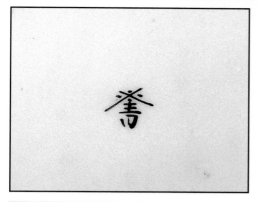

Fukagawa Porcelain Manufacturing Co., Ltd., Kan Yo Some Tsuke (Official Porcelain Underglaze Blue), various items of light tone blue porcelain designed by Iwao Fukagawa since 1977, blue.

Painted. A forgery of the Chinese mark of the Ching-noa period, A.D. 1465-1487.

Painted. A forgery of the Chinese mark of the Kea-tsing period, A.D. 1522-1566.

Sei Ji Kai Sha, the Company of Pure Water, established by the Fukagawa, Tsuji, Fukami, and Tezuka families, 1879-1883, red.

Painted on the finest "Old Japan" ware: *Sei nen Genki*, meaning, made in the Japanese period of Genki, A.D. 1570-1573.

Special Fukagawa decorated trademark with red river.

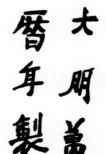

Painted. A forgery of the Chinese mark of the Wan-leih period, A.D. 1573-1619.

205

Painted on the finest "Old Japan" ware. A forgery of the Chinese mark of Kea-tsing period.

Painted on modern porcelain decorated in blue. *Sei nen Kea-tsing Tai Ming.* A forgery of the Chinese mark of the Kea-tsing period.

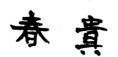

Painted on "Old Japan" ware. *Fuku Chio-shun*, meaning, Fortune and longevity.

Painted on a modern imitation of "Old Japan" ware. A forgery of the Chinese seal of the Keen-lung period, A.D. 1736-1795.

Painted, in the position shown, but in a complete circle. *Sei Ki-so Zo-moku an*, meaning made by Kiso at the factory of Zomokuan.

Painted on "Old Japan" ware of fair age and excellence. *Fuku*, meaning, Fortune and longevity.

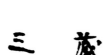

Painted on "Old Japan" ware of moderate excellence. *Zō Zo-shun-tei, San Ho*, meaning, made by San Ho at the factory of Zoshun.

Painte. *Zō Hi-guchi Nan-sen-zan,* meaning, made by Higuchi at the factory of Nansenzan.

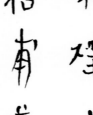

Painted. *Zō Ki-so Zo-moku-an*, meaning, made by Kiso at the factory of Zomokuan.

Painted on Nagasaki porcelain of moderate age and excellence. *Zō Hi-chio-zan Shin-po*, meaning, made by Hichiozan Shinpo.

Painted on modern porcelain decorated in blue.

Painted on modern Arita porcelain, *Sei Yamaka, Arita, Hizen*, meaning, made by Yamaka, at Artia, in Hizen.

Painted on modern porcelain decorated in colours and partially lacquered. *Sei Si-si Sai-sintei*, meaning, made by Sisi at the factory of Saisin.

Painted on modern Arita porcelain. *Zō Ki-so Zo-moku-an, Kankoro, Hizen*, meaning, made by Kiso at the factory of Zomokuan, in the public kiln of Hizen.

Painted on Nagasaki porcelain of the commonest description. A maker's mark.

Painted on modern porcelain decorated in colours and partially covered with *Cloisonné* enamel. *Zō Hi-chio-zan Shin-po, Dai Nippon*, meaning made by Hichiozan Shinpo, Great Japan.

Painted on Nagasaki porcelain of the commonest description. *Zō Hi-chio-zan Shin-sen*, meaning, made by Hichiozan Shinsen.

207

Hizen Province and Hirado Porcelain

Kaga Province and Kutani Porcelain

Made in the period 1804-1817. Found on Hirado porcelain.

  Mark used by Yeiraku (Zengoro Wazen) at Kutani in Great Japan, 1858-1864.

Made by Komoru at Mikawachi. Found on Hirado porcelain from 1870.

 Made by Yeiraku at Kutani 1858-1864.

Made at Hirado. Used since 1870.

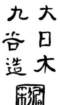 Made by Wakasugi at Kutani in Great Japan from 1779.

Made by Mori Chikara at Mikawachi since 1870.

  Various forms of ideograph Fuku (prosperity) written in gold, red, black or green enamel.

 Made by Farukawa at Mikawachi in Great Japan. Used since 1870.

  KUTANI (Nine Valleys) Old Style.

 KUTANI (Nine Valleys) New Style.

Painted. *Ku-tani, Hokufo*, the latter being the name of the maker; the square mark is the maker's monogram.

Painted. *Ku-tani, To-zan*, the latter being the name of the maker.

Painted on the choicest middle period ware. *To-zan*, Tozan being the name of the maker.

The word *Kutani*, meaning the Nine Valleys. These characters are generally painted upon Kaga ware, either alone or in combination with other marks.

Painted on choice middle period ware. *Kio-ku-zan, Kutani*, Kiokuzan being the name of the maker.

209

Painted on good middle period ware. *Dai Nip-pon*, *Ku-tani*, *Kachio ken*, *Sei*, meaning, made at the Kachio factory, Kutani, Great Japan.

Painted. *Dai Nip-pon*, *Ku-tani*, *Sei Kuroku ga*, meaning, made in Kutani, Great Japan, painted by Kuroku; the square mark is the monogram of Kuroku.

Painted on polychromatic ware. *Fuku*, meaning prosperity, luck, fortune, longevity, wealth and so forth.

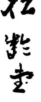

Painted on choice middle period ware. The two square characters are the monogram of Tozan, the maker, and the three upper marks signify *Shiorie do*, his professional name.

Painted on middle period ware. *Dai Nip-pon*, *Ku-tani*, *Zō Kio-ku-san*, meaning Great Japan, Kutani, made by Kiokuzan; the square character is the name of the maker.

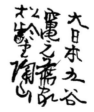

Painted on good late period ware. *Dai Nip-pon*, *Ku-tani*, *Kama-no-kin ka*, *Shio-rei do*, *To-zan*, meaning, that it was made by the old-established potter Shiorei do, Tozan, Kutani, Great Japan.

Painted on common modern porcelain. *Ku-tani Sei Itsu-kio do*, meaning, made in Kutani by Itsukio do.

Painted on late period ware. Beginning with the right-hand character, the inscription reads: *Dai Nip-pon*, *Ku-tani*, *Kinoshita Naomasa Sei*, meaning, made by Kinoshita Naomasa, in Kutani, Great Japan; the seal character is the monogram of the maker's professional name, Shiozo.

210

Painted on good late period ware. The characters in the centre are *Zō Yei-raku*; those to the left, *oite Ku-tani*; and those to the right, *Dai Nip-pon*, meaning, made by Yeiraku, in Kutani, Great Japan.

Painted on middle period ware. *Ku-tani*, *U-zan*, meaning, Uzan, the maker, Kutani.

Painted on late period ware. *Nip-pon*, *Ku-tani*, *U-zan Sei*, meaning, made by Uzan, Kutani, Japan.

Painted on choice late period ware. *Ku-tani*, *Sei-kan Zō*, meaning, made by Seikan, Kutani.

Painted on good middle period ware. *Ku-tani Sei*; it is not clear whether the lower character signifies the name of the maker or whether the mark should read – made in Kutani.

Painted on modern polychromatic ware of inferior character. *Ku-tani*, *Shio-zo*, Shiozo being the maker's name.

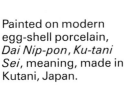

Painted on modern egg-shell porcelain, *Dai Nip-pon*, *Ku-tani Sei*, meaning, made in Kutani, Japan.

Painted on modern ware of inferior character. *Dai Nip-pon*, *Ku-tani*, *Tin-zan Zō*, meaning, made by Tinzan, Kutani, Great Japan; the character at the foot of the inscription is the monogram of the maker.

Painted on good late period ware. *Ku-tani*, *Iwazo Sei*, meaning, made by Iwazo, Kutani.

Painted on good middle period ware. *Kutani*, *Kio-ku zan Zō*, meaning, made by Kiokuzan, Kutani.

211

Kyoto Porcelain

Used by Mokubei at Awata b. 1707, d. 1833.

The Marks of Yeiraku Hozen, the Potter. 1801-1855.

Made by Yeiraku, beside the lake; Mark given him by Chief of Kisho, 1827, late 18th century

Made by Kyaraku (Mokubei), 18th century.

Mark of the Potter Hozen, late 18th century

Mokubei 1707-1833.

Made by Yeiraku (Wazen) of Great Japan from 1858

Mark of the Awata Kiln from 1765.

Mark used by Wazen 1858

Made by Shūhei, 18th century

SEI. Mark used by Rokubei, 1745-1799

Used by Shūhei or Hokkyo, 18th century

SEISAK. Mark used by Rekubei Gorosuke, 1811-1866

Made by Shūhei of Great Japan, 18th century

Mark used by Zengoro Hozen 1827-1844

Made by Shūhei, 18th century

Mark of Zoroku 1849-1878

The Marks of Yeiraku Hozen, the Potter. 1801-1855.

Seifu Yehei. Mark used by Seifu, 1844-1861

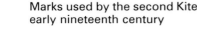

Marks used by the second Kitel, early nineteenth century

Painted on ware made during the first half of the eighteenth century by Shisui Kenzan of the Narutaki Kiln, in imitation of the celebrated productions of Nonomura Nensei. *Kenzan*, the name of the maker.

Impressed on *Raku* ware. *Raku*, meaning enjoyment, comfort, ease and pleasure.

Impressed. Another rendering of the word *Raku*

Painted on modern faïence of the most ordinary description. *Nip-pon, Kio-to, Kin Ko-zan Zō*, meaning, made by Kin Kozan, Kioto, Japan.

Another rendering of the word *Raku*.

Impressed. *Yei-raku*, the name of the maker.

Engraved. *Nagami Iwao Kore wo tsukuru*, meaning, Nagami Iwao made this.

Impressed. *Yei-raku*, the name of the maker.

Painted. *Zō Yei-raku, Kai Nip-pon*, meaning, made by Yeiraku, Great Japan.

Painted on Kyoto porcelain decorated in the *Kinrande* fashion. This mark is the same as the preceding one.

Impressed on *Raku* ware. *Kiu-raku*, the name of the maker.

213

Impressed on earthenware of great excellence. *Usetsu*, the name of the maker.

Impressed on earthenware of various kinds. *Tai-zan*, the name of the maker.

Impressed. *Tai-zan*, the name of the maker.

Impressed on earthenware of high class. *Tai-zan, Awata*, the name of the maker and of the district in which he resided.

Impressed. *Kin Ko-zan*, the name of the maker.

Painted upon earthenware of various kinds. *Sei Tan-zan, Nip-pon*, meaning, made by Tanzan, Japan.

Impressed on the highly-prized faïence made by Takahashi Dohachi about the year 1820. *Do-hachi*, the name of the maker.

Impressed on earthenware of fair style. *Bi-zan*, the name of the maker.

Impressed on faïence made by Nonomura Ninsei during the latter half of the seventeenth century. *Nin-sei*, the name of the maker. This mark was extensively forged in the late 19th century.

Impressed on common earthenware. *Matsu-moto*, the name of the maker.

Impressed on common earthenware. *Kin-un-ken*, the name of the factory.

Impressed on pottery. *Kio-midzu*, the name of one of the districts of Kioto in which pottery is made.

Painted on porcelain decorated in blue. *Dai Nip-pon, Shichi-bei Sei*, meaning, made by Shichibei, Great Japan.

Painted on modern pottery. *Zō Shu-hei, Dai Nip-pon*, meaning, made by Shuhei, Great Japan.

Kyoto Satsuma ware decorated by Yau Meizan.

Kyoto Satsuma decorated by Seikozan, late Edo or early Meiji.

Kyoto Satsuma decorated by Shoko Takabe, Thomas B. Blow.

Kyoto Satsuma decorated by Sozan in the Kinkozan workshop.

Owari Province and Seto Pottery

Painted on porcelain decorated in colours. *Dai Nip-pon*, *Roku-be-ye Sei*, meaning, made by Rokubeye, Great Japan.

Painted, in a recessed panel on a plaque. *Nippon*, *Se-to*, *Kawa-moto Masu-kichi Sei*, meaning, made by Kawamoto Masukichi, Seto, Japan.

Painted on porcelain decorated in colors. *O-chi Ken*, *Na-go-ya*, *Fuji-sima Sen-ta-ro Sei*, meaning, made by Fujisima Sentaro, Nagoya, Oehi Ken; the latter words probably are the name of the factory at which the ware was made.

215

Painted on porcelain decorated in blue. *Masukichi Sei*, meaning, made by Masukichi.

Impressed on porcelain decorated in the *Kinrande* fashion. *Yei-raku*, the name of the maker.

Painted on porcelain decorated in blue. *Masukichi Sei*, meaning, made by Masukichi.

Painted on porcelain decorated in blue. *Nip-pon, Se-to, Kawa-moto Han-suke Sei*, meaning, made by Kawamoto Hansuke, Seto, Japan.

Painted on porcelain decorated in blue. *Kawa-moto Masu-kichi sei, Sei*, meaning, made by Kawamoto Masukichi, best make.

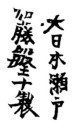

Painted on porcelain decorated in brown and blue. *Dai Nip-pon, Se-to, Ka-to Han-jen Sei*, meaning, made by Kato Hanjen, Seto, Great Japan.

Painted on porcelain decorated in colors. *Nip-pon, Se-to, Ka-to Kishi-ta-ro Lore wo tsukuru*, meaning, Kato Kishitaro made this at Seto, Japan.

Marks used by Kawamoto Hansuke at Seto in Japan about 1830.

Marks used by Kawamoto Hansuke at Seto in Japan about 1830.

Made at Seto in Great Japan.

Mark used by Gosuke at the Tagyokuyen.

SETOMONO

Satsuma Province and Satsuma Earthenware

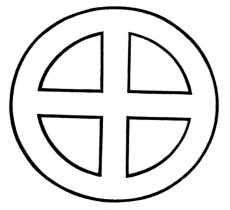

CREST OF THE PRINCE OF SAT-SUMA.

Painted. *Fu-ha-so-do Hitsu*, meaning, painted by Fuhaso do; the character at the foot is the painter's monogram.

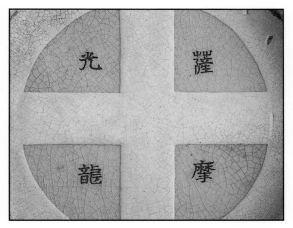

Mark reads Stasu Ma Ko Ryu, an export item made in Kagoshima Prefecture.

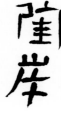

Engraved on earthenware of fair age. *To-gan*, the name of the maker.

Painted on the choicest faïence. *Ran-zan*, the name of the maker.

Painted on choice faïence. *Matsu-daira, Satsu-ma Kami*, being the name of the Prince of Satsuma, Matsudaira Satsuma no Kami.

Sumida ware by Hara Gozan

Sumida ware by Gozan

Sumida ware by Genlan Gozan

Sumida ware by Hara

Sumida ware by Genlan Gozan

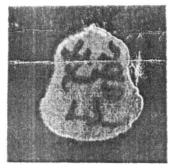

Sumida ware by Gozan

Sumida ware by Hara (phonetic)

Sumida ware by Gozan

Sumida ware by Hara

Sumida ware by Ishiguro Koko

Sumida ware by Koji/Koko

Dai Nippon (Great Japan) Tokyo, by Inoue Ryosai

Sumida ware by Koji/Koko

Inoue Ryosai

Sumida ware by Koko

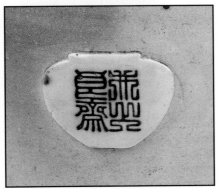

Inoue Ryosai

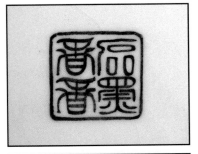

Ryosai

Sumida ware by Ishiguro Koko

Ryosai

Ryosai

Painted in Tokyo on porcelain made in Mino. The characters to the right signify *Tokio*, those in the cenetr state that the painting represents *A view of Atagoyama*, and the seal to the left is the monogram of the painter.

This mark is similar to that above, but the view represented is that of the Sumida river at Tokyo.

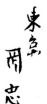

Painted on modern faïence. *To-kio, Okatada Zō*, meaning, made by Okatada, Tokyo.

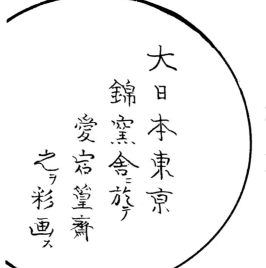

Painted on Hizen porcelain. *Dai Nippon, Tokio, Ginkoshia oite Otagi Kawsai saigas*, meaning, painted by Otagi Kowsai, in the Ginkoshia workshop, Tokyo, Great Japan.

Painted on modern faïence. *To-kio, Sei Simanchi Shin-zan ga*, meaning, made in Tokyo, painted by Simauchi Shinzan.

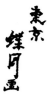

Painted *To-kio, Chogetsu ga*, meaning painted by Chogetsu, Tokyo.

Painted on egg-shell porcelain made at Arita. *To-kio, Yama-moto Shu-gets ga*, meaning, painted by Yamamoto Shugets, Tokyo.

Painted *To-kio, Matsumoto Ho-yen ga*, meaning, painted by Matsumoto Hoyen, Tokyo.

Painted on Owari porcelain. *To-kio, O-ka-wa, Ichi-raku ga*, meaning, painted by Okawa, Iehiraku, Tokyo; the character at the foot of the mark is the monogram of the painter.

Various Factories

Engraved on Bizen ware. *Kichi*, the name of the maker.

Engraved on Bizen ware. *Chio*, the name of the maker.

Painted on Mino porcelain. The mark of the maker.

Impressed on Idzumo faïence. *Ungsui*, the name of the maker.

Impressed on Asahi ware. *A sa-hi*, meaning, Morning light, the name by which the ware is known.

Impressed on Soma ware. *So-ma*, the name of the ware.

Impressed on Soma ware. *Kin-sige*, the name of the maker.

Impressed on Kishiu ware . *San-raku ken Sei*, meaning, made at the factory of Sanraku.

Impressed on choicest Celadon ware. *Nanki, Zui-si Dō*, meaning, made by Zuisi, in Nanki, which is the Chinese name for the province of Kii.

Painted on Aidtz porcelain. *Fosei ken Zō*, meaning, made at the factory of Fosei.

Impressed on Idsumi ware. *Senshu, Sa-kai, Hon Minato yaki Kichi-yemon*, meaning, Original Minato ware, made by Kechiyemon, Sakai in Senshu.

221

Bibliography

Audsley, George A. and James L. Bowes. *Keramic Art of Japan.* London: Henry Sotheran & Co., 1881.

Cardeiro, C. Philip. *Hirado Ware.* Monterey: Art Asia Museum, 1989.

Daruma Magazine, several editions. Higashi, Japan: Daruma Publishing, 1993-2001.

Earle, Joe. *Splendors of Meiji, Treasures of Imperial Japan, Masterpieces from the Khalili Collection.* St. Petersburg, Florida: Broughton International Publications, 1999.

Hackin, J. and others. *Asiatic Mythology.* New York: Crescent Books, 1963.

Lawrence, Louis. *Hirado: Prince of Porcelains, with an Introduction by David Hyatt King.* Chicago: Art Media Resources, Ltd. 1997.

_____*Satsuma, Masteroieces from the world's important Collections.* London: Dauphin Publishing Limited, 1991.

Levy, Mervyn. *Liberty Style, The Classic Years: 1898-1910.* New York: Rizzoli, 1986.

Mew, Egan. *Japanese Porcelain.* London: T. C. & E. C. Jack; and New York: Dodd Mead & Co., no date (about 1915).

Mitsuoka, Tadanari. *Ceramic Art of Japan.* Tokyo: Japan Travel Bureau, 1956.

Schiffer, Nancy N. *Imari, Satsuma, and other Japanese Export Ceramics*, Revised & Expanded 2nd edition. Atglen, Pennsylvania: Schiffer Publishing Ltd., 2000.

_____. *Japanese Export Ceramics 1860-1920.* Atglen, Pennsylvania: Schiffer Publishing Ltd., 2000.

_____. *Japanese Porcelain 1800-1950,* Expanded 2nd edition. Atglen, Pennsylvania: Schiffer Publishing Ltd., 1999.

Turk, Frank A. *The Prints of Japan.* New York: October House, 1966.

Watson, Eilliam, ed. *The Great Japan Exhibition, Art of the Edo Period 1600-1868.* London: Royal Academy of Arts and Weidenfeld and Nicolson, 1981.

Will, Captain John Baxter. *Trading Under Sail Off Japan, 1860-99, The Recollections of Captain John Baxter Will Sailing-master & Pilot edited with a Historical Introduction by George Alexander Lensen.* Tokyo: Sophia University in cooperation with The Diplomatic Press, Tallahassee, Florida, 1968.

Williams, C.A.S. *Outlines of Chinese Symbolism and Art Motives,* Third Revised Edition. Hong Kong: Kelly and Walsh, Limited.

Index

Arhats, 38

Asakusa, 12

shenaga, 71

anko pottery, 12

Benten, 15, 34, 35

Bijin, 137

Bing, Samuel, 7

Birds, 190-194

Bishamon, 15, 34-37

Bizen stoneware, 19

Boys, festival of, 100

British East India Co., 5,6

Carp, 195

Cats, 160-169

Clam, 195

Cocks, 191

Crab, 195, 198

Crane, 43

Daikoku, 9, 15, 17, 20, 24, 43, 96

Daruma, 38, 50-52

Dogs, 170

Dragons, 39, 90, 176, 198, 199

Ducks, 194

Dutch East India Co., 5

Eagles 194

Fish, 195, 197

Frog, 38, 41-43, 198

Fukagawa, 59

Fukurokuju, 15, 32, 33, 39

Gama-sennen, 38, 41-43

Girls, Feast of, 114

Girogin, 15-19, 33

Godo, Saijiro, 10

Hirado porcelain, 9, 11

Hizen province, 8

Ho-ho bird, 176, 194

Hongo pottery, 71

Horse, 174, 175

Hotei, 9, 15, 26-31, 98, 99

Imari porcelain, 8

Insects, 198

Ishiguro, Koko, 85

Iwashiro province, 71

Jinjukan, 11, 81-83, 110

Kabuki theater, 60-63

Kaga province, 10

Kaisai school, 7

Kannon, 38, 44-47, 199

Kan Wu, 11

Kirin, 176, 177

Kishimogin, 97

Koji, 192

Kutani porcelain, 10

Kylin, 176

Kyoto, 10, 11

Liberty, Arthur L., 7

Lion, 43, 175, 177

Makuzu, Kozan, 13

Mikado, 64, 65, 67

Mikawachi kiln, 9

Miyagawa, Kozan, 13

Monkey, 185

Nagami, Iwao, 19

Neo, 91

Octopus, 195
Ohokawachi stoneware, 43, 96
Okami, 38, 48, 49, 91, 114
Oni, 88, 89
Ota, 13
Otter, 188
Paris International Exhibition, 6, 13
Peacock, 190
Perry, Cdr. Matthew, 6
Pheasants, 190
Philadelphia Centennial Exhibition, 7, 13
Pig, 189
Plum,
Rabbit, 189
Rakon, 38
Reptiles, 198-200
Rooster, 191
Rypsai I, II, III, 12
Samurai, 66
Satsuma earthenware, 10
Sennen, 38, 39
Seto, 12
Seven gods of good fortune, 14-37
Shin-bei, 89
Shiou-Ro, 15-19

Shishi, 43, 175-184
Shoki, 88-96
Spider, 200
Streetsweepers, 68-70
Suma wrestlers, 84-86
Sumida pottery, 12
Suzuki, Yasubeye, 13
Taimano, Keimaya, 84
Takahashi, Dohachi, 33
Taizan, 113
Tenaga, 71
Tetsksai, 96
Thunder god ,38-41
Tiffany, Louis C., 7
Tokyo University, 7
Tortoise , 200
Toshi-Toku, 15, 32, 33
Van Gogh, Vincent, 7
Wagener, Dr. Gottfried, 6
Whistler, James McN., 7
Wilde, Oscar, 7
Yabu, Meizan, 162
Yebis, 15, 22-25
Yokohama, 13
Zodiac, 201